List of characters

The Court

HIPPOLYTA Queen of the Amazons, engaged to Theseus
THESEUS Duke of Athens, engaged to Hippolyta
EGEUS father of Hermia
PHILOSTRATE Master of the Revels to the Athenian Court

The lovers

HERMIA in love with Lysander
HELENA in love with Demetrius
LYSANDER in love with Hermia
DEMETRIUS Egeus's choice as a husband for Hermia

The Mechanicals
(workers who put on a play)

NICK BOTTOM a weaver who plays Pyramus
PETER QUINCE a carpenter who speaks the Prologue
FRANCIS FLUTE a bellows-mender who plays Thisbe
TOM SNOUT a tinker who plays Wall
ROBIN STARVELING a tailor who plays Moonshine
SNUG a joiner who plays Lion

The fairies

PUCK (or Robin Goodfellow) Oberon's attendant
OBERON King of the Fairies
TITANIA Queen of the Fairies
PEASEBLOSSOM ⎫
COBWEB ⎪
MOTH ⎬ Titania's fairy attendants
MUSTARDSEED ⎭
A FAIRY in Titania's service

Theseus, the Duke, and Hippolyta, Queen of the Amazons, speak about the preparations for their marriage in four days' time.

---

1 Theseus and Hippolyta (in pairs)

Shakespeare chooses to use characters from a myth well-known in his day. Theseus, the Duke of Athens, has fought a battle with the Amazons (a group of warrior women) and then married Hippolyta, their queen. Taking parts, read these speeches aloud, perhaps more than once. Then talk about what sort of relationship this seems to be. Try to find the key words or phrases in each speech, and then read just those. Then . . .

2 Another angle on the speeches (in the same pairs)

This time, look at the speeches on page 3 in terms of the key words and images, and see what patterns there are (like all those to do with the moon, or 'slow' versus 'quickly'). These patterns and the relationship between Theseus and Hippolyta give an idea of what the play will be about. Try to guess what might happen, and then share your ideas with another group.

3 Is there something wrong here? (in groups of four)

Taking parts (with one person as Philostrate and one as director/ audience), walk through this opening, trying to develop gestures and movements that fit the speeches. Try making one partner dominant and the other quiet (or even resentful). Have them in love and affectionate. Discuss which you like best, and why.

4 Moon, night and dreams (in groups of four)

Look at the title of the play and the first speeches. What kind of dream could this play be (a dream for the characters, or for the audience, or . . .)?

---

revenue wealth
solemnities formal ceremonies

CAMBRIDGE SCHOOL

Shakespeare

A Midsummer Night's Dream

Edited by Linda Buckle and Paul Kelley

Series Editor: Rex Gibson
Director, Shakespeare and Schools Project

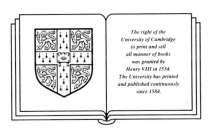

The right of the
University of Cambridge
to print and sell
all manner of books
was granted by
Henry VIII in 1534.
The University has printed
and published continuously
since 1584.

Cambridge   New York   Port Chester
Melbourne   Sydney

Published by the Press Syndicate of the University of Cambridge
The Pitt Building, Trumpington Street, Cambridge CB2 1RP
40 West 20th Street, New York, NY 10011–4211, USA
10 Stamford Road, Oakleigh, Victoria 3166, Australia

First published 1992

Printed in Great Britain at the University Press, Cambridge

British Library cataloguing in publication data
Shakespeare, William *1564–1616*
A midsummer night's dream. – (Cambridge School Shakespeare).
1. English drama
I. Title II. Buckle, Linda III. Kelley, Paul
822.33

ISBN 0 521 40904 7

Library of Congress cataloging in publication data
Shakespeare, William *1564–1616*
A midsummer night's dream/edited by Linda Buckle and Paul Kelley.
p. cm. – (Cambridge School Shakespeare)
Summary: An edition of Shakespeare's comedy, including discussion of its production, themes, patterns, language, and author.

ISBN 0 521 40904 7 (paper)

1. Young adult drama, English. [1. Shakespeare, William, 1564–1616. Midsummer night's dream. 2. Plays. 3. Shakespeare, William, 1564–1616 – Criticism and interpretation. 4. English literature – History and criticism.] I. Buckle, Linda. II. Kelley, Paul. III. Title. IV. Series: Shakespeare, William, 1564–1616. Works. 1991. Cambridge University Press.
PR2827.A25 1991
822.3′3 – dc20   91–26753
                                                                          CIP
                                                                          AC

Design by Richard Morris
Picture research by Callie Kendall

Thanks are due to the following for permission to reproduce photographs:

6, Photo courtesy of the Stratford Festival Archives; photographer: Zöe Dominic; Stratford Festival production, 1977; director Robin Philips, designer Susan Benson; 8, 58, 98, Shakespeare Centre Library: Thos. F. and Mig Holte Collection; 22, 36, 54, 76, 80, 100, 117, 140, © Robert Barber; 24, 66, Shakespeare Centre Library, Stratford-upon-Avon/photo: David Farrell; 25, 86, The New Shakespeare Company Ltd/photo: John Timbers; 32, 116, © BBC; 42, Royal Exchange Theatre, Manchester; 48, Bibliotheek der Rijksuniversiteit te Utrecht; 62, 74, 151, Shakespeare Centre Library, Stratford-upon-Avon; 88, B-11106 *Geschrei*, 1895, Edvard Munch 1863–1944, National Gallery of Art, Washington; Rosenwald Collection; 92, Alastair Muir; 114, 148, Hull Truck Theatre Company/photo: Steve Morgan; 120, The New Shakespeare Theatre Company Ltd/photo: Alastair Muir.

Contents

Cambridge School Shakespeare

This edition of *A Midsummer Night's Dream* is part of the *Cambridge School Shakespeare* series. Like every other play in the series, it has been specially prepared to help all students in schools and colleges.

This *A Midsummer Night's Dream* aims to be different from other editions of the play. It invites you to bring the play to life in your classroom, hall or drama studio through enjoyable activities that will increase your understanding. Actors have created their different interpretations of the play over the centuries. Similarly, you are encouraged to make up your own mind about *A Midsummer Night's Dream*, rather than having someone else's interpretation handed down to you.

Cambridge School Shakespeare does not offer you a cut-down or simplified version of the play. This is Shakespeare's language, filled with imaginative possibilities. You will find on every left-hand page: a summary of the action, an explanation of unfamiliar words, a choice of activities on Shakespeare's language, characters and stories.

Between each act and in the pages at the end of the play, you will find notes, illustrations and activities. These will help to increase your understanding of the whole play.

There are a large number of activities to give you the widest choice to suit your own particular needs. Please don't think you have to do every one. Choose the activities that will help you most.

This edition will be of value to you whether you are studying for an examination, reading for pleasure, or thinking of putting on the play to entertain others. You can work on the activities on your own or in groups. Many of the activities suggest a particular group size, but don't be afraid to make up larger or smaller groups to suit your own purposes.

Although you are invited to treat *A Midsummer Night's Dream* as a play, you don't need special dramatic or theatrical skills to do the activities. By choosing your activities, and by exploring and experimenting, you can make your own interpretations of Shakespeare's language, characters and stories. Whatever you do, remember that Shakespeare wrote his plays to be acted, watched and enjoyed.

Rex Gibson

This edition of *A Midsummer Night's Dream* uses the text of the play established by R. A. Foakes in *The New Cambridge Shakespeare*.

A Midsummer Night's Dream

ACT 1   SCENE 1
Athens   Theseus' Palace

Enter THESEUS, HIPPOLYTA, PHILOSTRATE, *with others*

THESEUS Now, fair Hippolyta, our nuptial hour
    Draws on apace; four happy days bring in
    Another moon – but O, methinks, how slow
    This old moon wanes! She lingers my desires,
    Like to a step-dame or a dowager   5
    Long withering out a young man's revenue.
HIPPOLYTA Four days will quickly steep themselves in night;
    Four nights will quickly dream away the time;
    And then the moon, like to a silver bow
    New bent in heaven, shall behold the night   10
    Of our solemnities.
THESEUS   Go, Philostrate,
    Stir up the Athenian youth to merriments,
    Awake the pert and nimble spirit of mirth;
    Turn melancholy forth to funerals;
    The pale companion is not for our pomp.   15
                      [Exit Philostrate]

    Hippolyta, I wooed thee with my sword,
    And won thy love doing thee injuries;
    But I will wed thee in another key,
    With pomp, with triumph, and with revelling.

Egeus enters with his daughter Hermia and the two men who wish to marry her, Lysander (whom she loves) and Demetrius (whom she dislikes). Egeus claims Lysander has 'bewitched' Hermia.

1 Acting and reacting (in groups of six)

There are a variety of different ways to act out this section. Act it emphasising the reactions of the lovers. Then discuss how relevant Egeus' sort of parental authority is today. Improvise this situation in small groups: parents attempt to enforce a ban on a girlfriend or boyfriend they disapprove of; or an arranged marriage is planned. Talk about the differences between Shakespeare's version and your own.

2 What do you think? (in groups of six)

Is Egeus being totally unreasonable, or is he a responsible Athenian father? Let one member of your group be Egeus and the rest a 'court'. Ask 'Egeus' questions and let him explain and defend his decision.

3 Egeus' speech (in pairs)

Divide Egeus' speech (lines 22–45) into different sections, perhaps according to whom he seems to be addressing at different times. Look at the differences in the language in each section. Try out different ways of speaking the lines, perhaps with a different person reading each section.

4 Love (in groups of four to six)

This is one of the harsher moments in the play: Egeus describes love as 'feigning' and 'cunning', and offers, as a solution, the strict brutality of the law. Talk about 'love' and what you think it is. Also talk about the problems it can cause, and what solutions there are. Write down your ideas and record other views of love as you come to them in the play.

---

feigning untrue, deceitful
gauds, conceits fancy trinkets

prevailment pressure
filched stolen

Enter EGEUS *and his daughter* HERMIA, LYSANDER *and* DEMETRIUS

EGEUS Happy be Theseus, our renownèd Duke!   20
THESEUS Thanks, good Egeus. What's the news with thee?
EGEUS Full of vexation come I, with complaint
        Against my child, my daughter Hermia.
        Stand forth, Demetrius! – My noble lord,
        This man hath my consent to marry her.   25
        Stand forth, Lysander! – And, my gracious Duke,
        This man hath bewitched the bosom of my child.
        Thou, thou, Lysander, thou hast given her rhymes,
        And interchanged love-tokens with my child.
        Thou hast by moonlight at her window sung   30
        With feigning voice verses of feigning love,
        And stolen the impression of her fantasy,
        With bracelets of thy hair, rings, gauds, conceits,
        Knacks, trifles, nosegays, sweetmeats – messengers
        Of strong prevailment in unhardened youth;   35
        With cunning hast thou filched my daughter's heart,
        Turned her obedience, which is due to me,
        To stubborn harshness. And, my gracious Duke,
        Be it so she will not here, before your grace,
        Consent to marry with Demetrius,   40
        I beg the ancient privilege of Athens;
        As she is mine, I may dispose of her;
        Which shall be either to this gentleman
        Or to her death, according to our law
        Immediately provided in that case.   45

Hermia refuses to marry Demetrius, despite the threat of being sent to a convent or being executed.

---

1 Parents (in groups of four to six)

Talk about what Theseus says on page 7, and what children owe to their parents. Consider the opposite view as well – parents are the biggest problem a child has to face as they grow to being an adult. Draw up a list of advantages and disadvantages of arranged marriages. Then look again at Hermia's decision: given the Athenian law, explain what you think of what she decides to do.

2 'Looked but with my eyes' (in groups of two to three)

Hermia means (line 56) she wishes Egeus could 'see' Lysander as she sees him. The people watching 'see' the debates on pages 7 and 9 very differently. Discuss what each one sees and why.

3 Male dominance? (in groups of four to six)

Already there has been a 'forced' engagement. Go through the script on pages 7 and 9 finding any images that imply male dominance, e.g. 'your father should be as a god'. Read the images about males, then those about females.

4 'Love' and 'dote'
(in groups of four to six)

On pages 7 and 9, there is a good deal of talk about feelings. Try to identify these different feelings and explain what they are. Talk about which characters are sensitive to other's feelings, and which are not.

Maggie Smith as Hippolyta.

---

imprinted moulded, stamped
livery clothes
mewed confined

barren sister nun
yoke constraint

THESEUS What say you, Hermia? Be advised, fair maid.
   To you your father should be as a god,
   One that composed your beauties; yea, and one
   To whom you are but as a form in wax
   By him imprinted, and within his power   50
   To leave the figure, or disfigure it.
   Demetrius is a worthy gentleman.
HERMIA So is Lysander.
THESEUS   In himself he is;
   But in this kind, wanting your father's voice,
   The other must be held the worthier.   55
HERMIA I would my father looked but with my eyes.
THESEUS Rather your eyes must with his judgement look.
HERMIA I do entreat your grace to pardon me.
   I know not by what power I am made bold,
   Nor how it may concern my modesty   60
   In such a presence here to plead my thoughts;
   But I beseech your grace that I may know
   The worst that may befall me in this case,
   If I refuse to wed Demetrius.
THESEUS Either to die the death, or to abjure   65
   For ever the society of men.
   Therefore, fair Hermia, question your desires,
   Know of your youth, examine well your blood,
   Whether, if you yield not to your father's choice,
   You can endure the livery of a nun,   70
   For aye to be in shady cloister mewed,
   To live a barren sister all your life,
   Chanting faint hymns to the cold fruitless moon.
   Thrice blessèd they that master so their blood
   To undergo such maiden pilgrimage;   75
   But earthlier happy is the rose distilled
   Than that which, withering on the virgin thorn,
   Grows, lives, and dies in single blessedness.
HERMIA So will I grow, so live, so die, my lord,
   Ere I will yield my virgin patent up   80
   Unto his lordship, whose unwishèd yoke
   My soul consents not to give sovereignty.

Theseus orders Hermia to make her decision before his wedding to Hippolyta. Lysander argues his case and points out Demetrius loved Helena before Hermia.

Theseus and Hermia (Royal Shakespeare Company, 1962).

austerity self-control, abstinence
estate unto give to

well-derived of a good family and background

THESEUS Take time to pause, and by the next new moon,
The sealing-day betwixt my love and me
For everlasting bond of fellowship, 85
Upon that day either prepare to die
For disobedience to your father's will,
Or else to wed Demetrius, as he would,
Or on Diana's altar to protest
For aye austerity and single life. 90
DEMETRIUS Relent, sweet Hermia; and, Lysander, yield
Thy crazèd title to my certain right.
LYSANDER You have her father's love, Demetrius;
Let me have Hermia's – do you marry him.
EGEUS Scornful Lysander, true, he hath my love, 95
And what is mine my love shall render him;
And she is mine, and all my right of her
I do estate unto Demetrius.
LYSANDER I am, my lord, as well-derived as he,
As well-possessed: my love is more than his, 100
My fortunes every way as fairly ranked,
If not with vantage, as Demetrius';
And, which is more than all these boasts can be,
I am beloved of beauteous Hermia.
Why should not I then prosecute my right? 105
Demetrius, I'll avouch it to his head,
Made love to Nedar's daughter, Helena,
And won her soul; and she, sweet lady, dotes,
Devoutly dotes, dotes in idolatry,
Upon this spotted and inconstant man. 110

Theseus warns Hermia, and takes Demetrius and Egeus away to talk to them. Left alone, Lysander and Hermia discuss the problems of lovers.

---

1 Hippolyta speaks (in pairs)

Hippolyta remains silent throughout this extremely emotional debate about Hermia. She and Theseus leave together. They are about to be married. Improvise the conversation they may have about what has just happened, what each thinks of the situation and the characters involved, and bear in mind how Hippolyta might relate to Hermia's plight and Theseus' judgement.

2 Love – 'short as any dream' (in groups of two to three)

Look through Lysander's speech here (lines 141–9) where he paints love as a temporary thing ('momentany', 'swift', 'short', 'brief'), surrounded by a hostile world. Talk about what he compares love to, and whether you think the comparisons are suitable.

3 'The course of true love never did run smooth' (in groups of two to three)

This phrase (line 134) has become a commonplace saying. How true is it? Think about what it might be implying about the rest of the play.

4 The dance of the lovers – who loves whom?

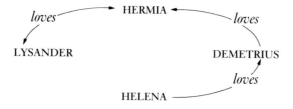

---

against in preparation for
beteem grant
blood class, family background
enthralled bound

misgraffèd mismatched
collied darkened, like coal
spleen burst of temper

THESEUS I must confess that I have heard so much,
And with Demetrius thought to have spoke thereof;
But, being overfull of self-affairs,
My mind did lose it. But Demetrius, come,
And come, Egeus. You shall go with me;   115
I have some private schooling for you both.
For you, fair Hermia, look you arm yourself
To fit your fancies to your father's will;
Or else the law of Athens yields you up
(Which by no means we may extenuate)   120
To death, or to a vow of single life.
Come, my Hippolyta; what cheer, my love?
Demetrius and Egeus, go along;
I must employ you in some business
Against our nuptial, and confer with you   125
Of something nearly that concerns yourselves.
EGEUS With duty and desire we follow you.

                    Exeunt all but Lysander and Hermia

LYSANDER How now, my love? Why is your cheek so pale?
How chance the roses there do fade so fast?
HERMIA Belike for want of rain, which I could well   130
Beteem them from the tempest of my eyes.
LYSANDER Ay me! For aught that I could ever read,
Could ever hear by tale or history,
The course of true love never did run smooth;
But either it was different in blood –   135
HERMIA O cross! too high to be enthralled to low.
LYSANDER Or else misgraffèd in respect of years –
HERMIA O spite! too old to be engaged to young.
LYSANDER Or else it stood upon the choice of friends –
HERMIA O hell, to choose love by another's eyes!   140
LYSANDER Or, if there were a sympathy in choice,
War, death, or sickness did lay siege to it,
Making it momentany as a sound,
Swift as a shadow, short as any dream,
Brief as the lightning in the collied night,   145
That in a spleen unfolds both heaven and earth,
And, ere a man hath power to say 'Behold!',
The jaws of darkness do devour it up.
So quick bright things come to confusion.

Lysander and Hermia plan to elope.
They arrange to meet 'tomorrow night' in the wood outside the city.

---

1 Running away (in small groups)

Begin by talking about running away from problems, and running away as a couple. Is it ever a wise move? Look at Lysander and Hermia's situation and discuss the different options the lovers have and which is wisest.

2 'Teach our trial patience' (in pairs)

Hermia suggests (line 152) they be patient, and Lysander agrees ('a good persuasion'), but then he suggests they run away. The two lovers (and especially Hermia here) seem to swing from one mood to another. Find a space and act out these lines, trying to bring out the moods of each character by what they do, and how they speak.

3 What 'dream'? (in groups four to six)

Hermia speaks of features of love like thoughts and wishes and dreams. Talk about what sort of dreams lovers have, especially these two (being together, freedom from restrictions, happiness, sex . . .). She also swears oaths by the goddess of love (Venus) and other lovers (Dido, Queen of Carthage who loved Aeneas, the false Trojan). Love, for Hermia, is like a dream she lives in all the time. Is this what love is like?

4 'These visions did appear' (in groups of four to six)

Look at some of the photographs of how the play has been produced (pages 8, 22, and 24, for example). After talking about the sets, costumes, and how the characters are presented, design your own poster for display in the classroom.

---

edict command
revenue wealth
league about three miles

HERMIA If then true lovers have been ever crossed   150
It stands as an edict in destiny.
Then let us teach our trial patience,
Because it is a customary cross,
As due to love as thoughts, and dreams, and sighs,
Wishes, and tears – poor fancy's followers.   155
LYSANDER A good persuasion. Therefore hear me, Hermia:
I have a widow aunt, a dowager,
Of great revenue, and she hath no child.
From Athens is her house remote seven leagues;
And she respects me as her only son.   160
There, gentle Hermia, may I marry thee;
And to that place the sharp Athenian law
Cannot pursue us. If thou lov'st me, then
Steal forth thy father's house tomorrow night,
And in the wood, a league without the town   165
(Where I did meet thee once with Helena
To do observance to a morn of May),
There will I stay for thee.
HERMIA   My good Lysander,
I swear to thee by Cupid's strongest bow,
By his best arrow with the golden head,   170
By the simplicity of Venus' doves,
By that which knitteth souls and prospers loves,
And by that fire which burned the Carthage queen
When the false Trojan under sail was seen,
By all the vows that ever men have broke   175
(In number more than ever women spoke),
In that same place thou hast appointed me,
Tomorrow truly will I meet with thee.
LYSANDER Keep promise, love. Look, here comes Helena.

*Helena enters, talking of Demetrius' love for Hermia (who rejects him).
Lysander tells her of the plan to elope.*

---

1 What do you make of Helena? (in pairs)

Read through the scene between Helena and Hermia (lines 180–
207), then talk about Helena and her situation. Look through her
speeches again, and try to find key words and phrases that bring out
her character. You could read these aloud. Act out these lines
emphasising those key words and phrases. What do you feel about
Helena?

2 Another fine mess you've got us into, William
   (in groups of four to six)

Shakespeare seems to have begun his play by setting up an extremely
difficult situation for his lovers (remember that Helena is in love too,
even if her love is not returned). If the play is a comedy, in the sense
that there is a happy ending for all the lovers, it's a bit hard to see how
it will happen. Invent a variety of different plots that might bring them
all together at the end.

3 Looking for patterns (in pairs)

Poetry is a kind of patterned speech or writing. You've probably
noticed how the play is in blank verse and couplets so far (even if you
didn't know the name of this kind of poetry). But Shakespeare also
uses other patterns. Look carefully at lines 194–201 and see what
kinds of patterns you can find in this conversation.

4 'Seemed Athens as a paradise to me' (in groups of four)

Hermia says her feelings about Athens have completely changed (line
205). From what you know so far, decide whether Athens is a
'heaven' or a 'hell', and whether you would like to live in that kind of
world.

---

lodestars guiding star
bated excepted

Phoebe Diana, goddess of the
moon, associated with chastity

Enter HELENA

HERMIA God speed, fair Helena! Whither away?   180
HELENA Call you me fair? That 'fair' again unsay.
       Demetrius loves your fair: O happy fair!
       Your eyes are lodestars, and your tongue's sweet air
       More tuneable than lark to shepherd's ear
       When wheat is green, when hawthorn buds appear.   185
       Sickness is catching. O, were favour so,
       Yours would I catch, fair Hermia, ere I go;
       My ear should catch your voice, my eye your eye,
       My tongue should catch your tongue's sweet melody.
       Were the world mine, Demetrius being bated,   190
       The rest I'd give to be to you translated.
       O, teach me how you look, and with what art
       You sway the motion of Demetrius' heart.
HERMIA I frown upon him; yet he loves me still.
HELENA O that your frowns would teach my smiles such skill!   195
HERMIA I give him curses; yet he gives me love.
HELENA O that my prayers could such affection move!
HERMIA The more I hate, the more he follows me.
HELENA The more I love, the more he hateth me.
HERMIA His folly, Helena, is no fault of mine.   200
HELENA None but your beauty; would that fault were mine!
HERMIA Take comfort: he no more shall see my face;
       Lysander and myself will fly this place.
       Before the time I did Lysander see,
       Seemed Athens as a paradise to me.   205
       O then, what graces in my love do dwell,
       That he hath turned a heaven unto a hell?
LYSANDER Helen, to you our minds we will unfold:
       Tomorrow night, when Phoebe doth behold
       Her silver visage in the watery glass,   210
       Decking with liquid pearl the bladed grass
       (A time that lovers' flights doth still conceal),
       Through Athens' gates have we devised to steal.

Hermia and Lysander leave, wishing Helena luck in love. Helena reflects on the nature of love, and decides to tell Demetrius of the elopement.

1 The lovers (in groups of three to four)

This scene ends with Helena's decision to tell Demetrius about the elopement, which can only lead to trouble. Discuss the four lovers separately, as they have appeared in this scene, trying to bring out what you think of each. Think in terms of the different relationships (Hermia and Helena, Hermia and Demetrius and so on). Consider how they are different and how the same, and which you like best (and least).

2 Looking back (in groups of three to four)

Hermia talks of her past times with Helena ('where often you and I . . .'). Imagine what might have occurred in the past two months leading up to this first scene – meetings between any of the lovers, incidents, conversations or arguments, and so on. Pick one or two and improvise them. Show your favourite to the class as a whole.

3 Love – Helena's view (in groups of three to four)

Helena explains what she thinks of love in lines 232–9, using a comparison with Cupid (the mythical god of love, a young child with wings, who was sometimes presented as being blind). Work carefully through these lines, two lines at a time, until you're sure of what she's saying (ask for help if you need it). Discuss whether Helena's view is true of the other lovers, and of lovers that you know.

---

holding no quantity having no value
beguiled tricked
waggish mischievous
eyne eyes

HERMIA   And in the wood, where often you and I
Upon faint primrose beds were wont to lie,   215
Emptying our bosoms of their counsel sweet,
There my Lysander and myself shall meet,
And thence from Athens turn away our eyes
To seek new friends and stranger companies.
Farewell, sweet playfellow; pray thou for us,   220
And good luck grant thee thy Demetrius.
Keep word, Lysander; we must starve our sight
From lovers' food till morrow deep midnight.
LYSANDER   I will, my Hermia.

Exit Hermia

Helena, adieu!
As you on him, Demetrius dote on you.   *Exit Lysander*   225
HELENA   How happy some o'er other some can be!
Through Athens I am thought as fair as she.
But what of that? Demetrius thinks not so;
He will not know what all but he do know.
And as he errs, doting on Hermia's eyes,   230
So I, admiring of his qualities.
Things base and vile, holding no quantity,
Love can transpose to form and dignity.
Love looks not with the eyes, but with the mind,
And therefore is winged Cupid painted blind.   235
Nor hath love's mind of any judgement taste;
Wings, and no eyes, figure unheedy haste;
And therefore is love said to be a child
Because in choice he is so oft beguiled.
As waggish boys in game themselves forswear,   240
So the boy Love is perjured everywhere;
For, ere Demetrius looked on Hermia's eyne,
He hailed down oaths that he was only mine,
And when this hail some heat from Hermia felt,
So he dissolved, and showers of oaths did melt.   245
I will go tell him of fair Hermia's flight:
Then to the wood will he, tomorrow night,
Pursue her; and for this intelligence,
If I have thanks it is a dear expense;
But herein mean I to enrich my pain,   250
To have his sight thither, and back again.   *Exit*

A group of workers (the Mechanicals) – Quince, Snug, Bottom, Flute, Snout, and Starveling – meet to prepare a play for the Duke's wedding.

---

1 Who have we here? (in groups of six)

Shakespeare gives these characters distinctive names and trades. As a group, look at each one in turn, and how the name and trade helps establish their character. Choose a character, and work for a little while on your own, reading your character's lines and thinking about how to develop your part. Come back together to read through and act out this scene. You might like to keep together as a team for the Mechanicals' sections of the play.

2 We've hit Bottom (in groups of six)

Everyone knows a Bottom-like character – perhaps there is even one in your group. Talk about what you think of Bottom (and what the other Mechanicals think of him). He is one of the most popular of all of Shakespeare's characters, despite his being so completely over-the-top – why might this be?

3 Who have we here? (2) (in groups of six)

The Mechanicals, as a group, are a real contrast with the mythical Court of Athens, if only because they are so definitely of Shakespeare's time and place. Talk about the differences, and why Shakespeare might have included the Mechanicals and their very different world.

4 The Mechanicals' language (in groups of two to three)

Compare the Mechanicals' language to that of the Court (the way they speak, the words they use, and so on). As you go along, see how many contradictions ('wedding day at night') and other silly things they say you can find. Read them out.

---

condole show grief
Ercles Hercules
to tear a cat in to rant and rave. What kind of acting is Bottom used to, and what kind of play?

Phibbus Phoebus, god of the sun, who was supposed to drive a chariot ('car') through the sky

ACT 1 SCENE 2
Athens

Enter QUINCE the Carpenter, and SNUG the Joiner, and BOTTOM the
Weaver, and FLUTE the Bellows-mender, and SNOUT the Tinker and
STARVELING the Tailor

QUINCE Is all our company here?

BOTTOM You were best to call them generally, man by man, according
to the scrip.

QUINCE Here is the scroll of every man's name which is thought fit
through all Athens to play in our interlude before the Duke and   5
the Duchess on his wedding day at night.

BOTTOM First, good Peter Quince, say what the play treats on; then
read the names of the actors; and so grow to a point.

QUINCE Marry, our play is 'The most lamentable comedy and most
cruel death of Pyramus and Thisbe'.   10

BOTTOM A very good piece of work, I assure you, and a merry. Now,
good Peter Quince, call forth your actors by the scroll. Masters,
spread yourselves.

QUINCE Answer as I call you. Nick Bottom, the weaver?

BOTTOM Ready. Name what part I am for, and proceed.   15

QUINCE You, Nick Bottom, are set down for Pyramus.

BOTTOM What is Pyramus? A lover or a tyrant?

QUINCE A lover that kills himself, most gallant, for love.

BOTTOM That will ask some tears in the true performing of it. If I do
it, let the audience look to their eyes: I will move storms, I will   20
condole, in some measure. To the rest – yet my chief humour is
for a tyrant. I could play Ercles rarely, or a part to tear a cat in,
to make all split:

> The raging rocks
> And shivering shocks   25
> Shall break the locks
>   Of prison gates,
> And Phibbus' car
> Shall shine from far,
> And make and mar   30
>   The foolish Fates.

Quince assigns parts to each of the Mechanicals. Bottom volunteers to play two roles, but Quince says no.

---

1 'A monstrous little voice' (in groups of six)

The problem of Flute playing a woman (lines 42–3) is partly solved, so the Mechanicals believe, by Flute speaking in a high-pitched voice. Discuss how each of the Mechanicals might speak normally, and then try out different voices for each (different accents, speed, and so on).

2 'Let me not play a woman' (in groups of six)

On Shakespeare's stage, all the actors were men. Prepare and then act out for the rest of the class this scene (1.2) played by all women, and 1.1.180–224 (pages 15–17) by all men. How do you react as an audience?

3 The Mechanicals' play (in groups of two to three)

The Mechanicals' play changes a lot before it is finally acted. Using the description in this scene improvise – or write and perform – the play as you think it might have been. Compare your version with the final version in Act 5.

4 Believe a play? (in groups of two to three)

The Mechanicals seem to think that if Bottom played the lion's part he would frighten the women in the audience (lines 60–63 on page 23). What does this tell you about the Mechanicals and how they think about plays?

5 'These visions did appear' (in groups of two to three)

Look carefully at some of the photographs of the Mechanicals in various productions (see pages 22, 114 and 116). Explain which version you like best, and which least, and why.

---

small high-pitched

This was lofty. Now name the rest of the players. – This is Ercles'
vein, a tyrant's vein; a lover is more condoling.

QUINCE Francis Flute, the bellows-mender?

FLUTE Here, Peter Quince.   35

QUINCE Flute, you must take Thisbe on you.

FLUTE What is Thisbe? A wandering knight?

QUINCE It is the lady that Pyramus must love.

FLUTE Nay, faith, let not me play a woman: I have a beard coming.

QUINCE That's all one: you shall play it in a mask, and you may speak   40
as small as you will.

BOTTOM And I may hide my face, let me play Thisbe too. I'll speak
in a monstrous little voice: 'Thisne, Thisne!' – 'Ah, Pyramus, my
lover dear; thy Thisbe dear, and lady dear.'

QUINCE No, no; you must play Pyramus; and Flute, you Thisbe.   45

BOTTOM Well, proceed.

QUINCE Robin Starveling, the tailor?

STARVELING Here, Peter Quince.

QUINCE Robin Starveling, you must play Thisbe's mother. Tom Snout,
the tinker?   50

SNOUT Here, Peter Quince.

QUINCE You, Pyramus' father; myself, Thisbe's father; Snug, the
joiner, you the lion's part; and I hope here is a play fitted.

*Quince completes the arrangements for the play despite
Bottom's interruptions. They plan to meet in the wood 'tomorrow night'.*

The Mechanicals (Renaissance Theatre Company, 1990).

extempore ad lib
con learn
be dogged with company have
  people watching

SNUG Have you the lion's part written? Pray you, if it be, give it me;
for I am slow of study.   55

QUINCE You may do it extempore; for it is nothing but roaring.

BOTTOM Let me play the lion too. I will roar that I will do any man's
heart good to hear me. I will roar that I will make the Duke say
'Let him roar again, let him roar again!'

QUINCE And you should do it too terribly, you would fright the   60
Duchess and the ladies that they would shriek; and that were
enough to hang us all.

ALL That would hang us, every mother's son.

BOTTOM I grant you, friends, if you should fright the ladies out of their
wits they would have no more discretion but to hang us; but I will   65
aggravate my voice so that I will roar you as gently as any sucking
dove. I will roar you and 'twere any nightingale.

QUINCE You can play no part but Pyramus; for Pyramus is a sweet-faced
man, a proper man as one shall see in a summer's day, a most lovely,
gentlemanlike man: therefore you must needs play Pyramus.   70

BOTTOM Well, I will undertake it. What beard were I best to play it
in?

QUINCE Why, what you will.

BOTTOM I will discharge it in either your straw-colour beard, your
orange-tawny beard, your purple-in-grain beard, or your French-   75
crown-colour beard, your perfect yellow.

QUINCE Some of your French crowns have no hair at all, and then you
will play bare-faced. But, masters, here are your parts, and I am
to entreat you, request you, and desire you to con them by
tomorrow night, and meet me in the palace wood, a mile without   80
the town, by moonlight; there will we rehearse, for if we meet in
the city we shall be dogged with company, and our devices known.
In the meantime I will draw a bill of properties, such as our play
wants. I pray you, fail me not.

BOTTOM We will meet, and there we may rehearse most obscenely and   85
courageously. Take pains, be perfect: adieu!

QUINCE At the Duke's oak we meet.

BOTTOM Enough; hold, or cut bowstrings.

Exeunt

A Midsummer Night's Dream

Titania and the fairies (Royal Shakespeare Company, 1970).

Titania and Oberon (New Shakespeare Company, 1971).

A fairy and Puck meet, and Puck explains the conflict between the King and Queen of the Fairies, Oberon and Titania.

1 The fairy world (1) (in pairs)

This is another world introduced into the play. Build up an idea of what sort of world it is by sketching the images from the fairy's speech (lines 2–17). Compare this world with the world (or worlds) of the first act, including similarities such as the love conflict.

2 The fairy world (2) (in pairs)

Act out this passage, working on the gestures and movements that would bring out the world of the fairies as you think it should be. Compare these characters with the Mechanicals, and the Athenian Court.

3 What do we see? (in groups of four)

Both speeches create visions (or dreams) in the audience's mind of things that happen in the fairy world. Some images would be very difficult to put on a stage (e.g. 'elves for fear/Creep into acorn cups'). Discuss how much help the audience needs to imagine what is described (this scene is set at night in a wood). You could be like the Mechanicals – very literal in trying to present everything – or leave it all to the power of Shakespeare's language (see pages 36–7).

4 'These visions did appear' (in groups of four)

The problems of presenting the fairy world on stage have been solved in very different ways (see pages 24, 25, 32, and 36). Design your own fairy world and costumes. You could experiment with the idea of using light and shadow, or even puppets.

---

lob lout
passing . . . wrath very fierce and angry

changeling a child stolen by fairies
square quarrel

ACT 2   SCENE 1
The wood

Enter a FAIRY *at one door, and* PUCK, *or* ROBIN GOODFELLOW
at another

PUCK How now, spirit; whither wander you?
FAIRY Over hill, over dale,
    Thorough bush, thorough briar,
   Over park, over pale,
    Thorough flood, thorough fire;   5
   I do wander everywhere
   Swifter than the moon's sphere;
   And I serve the Fairy Queen,
   To dew her orbs upon the green.
   The cowslips tall her pensioners be; 10
   In their gold coats spots you see –
   Those be rubies, fairy favours,
   In those freckles live their savours.
    I must go seek some dewdrops here,
    And hang a pearl in every cowslip's ear. 15
  Farewell, thou lob of spirits; I'll be gone.
  Our Queen and all her elves come here anon.
PUCK The King doth keep his revels here tonight.
  Take heed the Queen come not within his sight,
  For Oberon is passing fell and wrath,   20
  Because that she as her attendant hath
  A lovely boy stol'n from an Indian king;
  She never had so sweet a changeling,
  And jealous Oberon would have the child
  Knight of his train, to trace the forests wild. 25
  But she perforce withholds the lovèd boy,
  Crowns him with flowers, and makes him all her joy.
  And now they never meet in grove or green,
  By fountain clear or spangled starlight sheen,
  But they do square, that all their elves for fear 30
  Creep into acorn cups and hide them there.

Puck and the fairy talk about the sort of 'sprite' Puck is.

---

1 Puck (in groups of three to four)

Puck is one of Shakespeare's best-known characters, and both speeches serve to introduce him to the audience. Make a list of the adjectives used to describe him ('shrewd' and so on), and a list of what he is described as doing. Using both lists, describe what kind of character he is. You can add to your lists as you continue reading the play.

2 Speech and actions (in pairs)

Take turns reading Puck's speech (lines 43–58) and fit actions to it, miming some of the things he talks about.

3 What do we see? (in groups of three to four)

Look at some of the photographs from productions (pages 36, 42, 74 and 148). Discuss each one, commenting on why Puck looks the way he does. There's one surprise here, isn't there?

4 Just to think about

This quotation comes from a book Shakespeare probably read called *The Discovery of Witchcraft* (it was written in 1584):

> 'Indeed your grandams' maids set a bowl of milk out for Robin Goodfellow . . . the mare, the man in the oak, the puckle, hobgoblin'.

The book also describes incidents similar to those the fairy and Puck talk about, but, as the quotation implies, the author said hardly anyone believed in Puck or Robin Goodfellow any more. Why does Shakespeare use so many imaginary characters from myth and superstition in the play?

---

shrewd evil or mischievous: which do you think suits him best in his own description of himself?
skim milk skim off the cream
quern hand mill for grinding corn
bootless pointless
barm the head on beer
crab crab apple
loffe laugh

FAIRY   Either I mistake your shape and making quite,
          Or else you are that shrewd and knavish sprite
          Called Robin Goodfellow. Are not you he
          That frights the maidens of the villagery,   35
          Skim milk, and sometimes labour in the quern,
          And bootless make the breathless housewife churn,
          And sometime make the drink to bear no barm,
          Mislead night-wanderers, laughing at their harm?
          Those that 'Hobgoblin' call you, and 'Sweet Puck',   40
          You do their work, and they shall have good luck.
          Are not you he?
PUCK   Thou speakest aright;
          I am that merry wanderer of the night.
          I jest to Oberon, and make him smile
          When I a fat and bean-fed horse beguile,   45
          Neighing in likeness of a filly foal;
          And sometime lurk I in a gossip's bowl
          In very likeness of a roasted crab,
          And when she drinks, against her lips I bob,
          And on her withered dewlap pour the ale.   50
          The wisest aunt, telling the saddest tale,
          Sometime for threefoot stool mistaketh me;
          Then slip I from her bum, down topples she,
          And 'Tailor' cries, and falls into a cough;
          And then the whole choir hold their hips and loffe,   55
          And waxen in their mirth, and neeze, and swear
          A merrier hour was never wasted there.
          But room, Fairy: here comes Oberon.
FAIRY   And here my mistress. Would that he were gone!

Oberon and Titania enter with their attendants. They accuse each other of being attracted to the mortals, Theseus and Hippolyta.

---

1 Nice to meet you (in pairs)

Read through these speeches aloud, and then talk about what each character is feeling at different points in the confrontation. As you read them through again, try to bring out these feelings by using different tones: angry, sarcastic or whatever you feel is right.

2 The relationship (in groups of four to six)

Discuss the relationship between Titania and Oberon here, and the sexual nature of their conversation. This is another conflict between lovers. Talk about any parallels with the relationships in the first act, and what sort of mood it creates in the play here. Then discuss the last lines of Titania's speech on page 33 (lines 115–7), and what they imply about the importance of Oberon and Titania's relationship.

3 Watch your language (in groups of two to three)

Our world is always changing, and so is our language. You can see some of these changes by comparing Shakespeare's language with the way we speak and write today. Use Titania's speech on page 33 (lines 81–117). First look for evidence of an older way of life ('ox ... stetched his yoke') or belief ('contagious fogs'). You can see how writing about an older way of life naturally means using different language. Then look for words we no longer use today. Finally, look for uses of language that are distinctive because this is poetry. Titania's speech concerns the disruption of the natural world because of the conflict between her and Oberon (this says something about their power in and over nature). Write another speech (once in prose, once in verse) about a similar problem of today, global warming. Compare your use of language with Shakespeare's.

---

tarry wait
lord, lady they are husband and wife
Corin, Phillida two mythical lovers

buskined wearing hunting boots
Perigenia, Aegles, Ariadne, Antiopa women Theseus slept with

Enter OBERON *the King of Fairies, at one door, with his train; and*
TITANIA, *the Queen, at another with hers*

OBERON   Ill met by moonlight, proud Titania!   60
TITANIA   What, jealous Oberon? Fairies, skip hence.
        I have forsworn his bed and company.
OBERON   Tarry, rash wanton! Am not I thy lord?
TITANIA   Then I must be thy lady. But I know
        When thou hast stol'n away from Fairyland,   65
        And in the shape of Corin sat all day
        Playing on pipes of corn, and versing love
        To amorous Phillida. Why art thou here
        Come from the farthest step of India? –
        But that, forsooth, the bouncing Amazon,   70
        Your buskined mistress and your warrior love,
        To Theseus must be wedded; and you come
        To give their bed joy and prosperity.
OBERON   How canst thou thus, for shame, Titania,
        Glance at my credit with Hippolyta,   75
        Knowing I know thy love to Theseus?
        Didst not thou lead him through the glimmering night
        From Perigenia, whom he ravishèd,
        And make him with fair Aegles break his faith,
        With Ariadne, and Antiopa?   80

Titania says the dispute with Oberon has changed the natural patterns of the climate and the seasons.

Oberon (BBC, 1981).

---

ringlets dancing in a circle
murrion flock diseased sheep
distemperature disorder
old Hiems winter

childing pregnant, fruitful
mazèd amazed, confused: a word used frequently in the play

TITANIA These are the forgeries of jealousy:
And never since the middle summer's spring
Met we on hill, in dale, forest, or mead,
By pavèd fountain or by rushy brook,
Or in the beachèd margent of the sea   85
To dance our ringlets to the whistling wind,
But with thy brawls thou hast disturbed our sport.
Therefore the winds, piping to us in vain,
As in revenge have sucked up from the sea
Contagious fogs; which, falling in the land,   90
Hath every pelting river made so proud
That they have overborne their continents.
The ox hath therefore stretched his yoke in vain,
The ploughman lost his sweat, and the green corn
Hath rotted ere his youth attained a beard.   95
The fold stands empty in the drownèd field,
And crows are fatted with the murrion flock;
The nine-men's-morris is filled up with mud,
And the quaint mazes in the wanton green
For lack of tread are undistinguishable.   100
The human mortals want their winter cheer;
No night is now with hymn or carol blessed.
Therefore the moon, the governess of floods,
Pale in her anger, washes all the air,
That rheumatic diseases do abound;   105
And thorough this distemperature we see
The seasons alter; hoary-headed frosts
Fall in the fresh lap of the crimson rose,
And on old Hiems' thin and icy crown
An odorous chaplet of sweet summer buds   110
Is, as in mockery, set. The spring, the summer,
The childing autumn, angry winter change
Their wonted liveries, and the mazèd world
By their increase now knows not which is which.
And this same progeny of evils comes   115
From our debate, from our dissension.
We are their parents and original.

Oberon asks Titania to give up her 'changeling boy', the subject of the quarrel. She explains she is going to keep him, and Oberon promises to be revenged.

1 Titania (in groups of four)

Look carefully at Titania's reasons for keeping the boy, deciding whether or not she is right. Once again in the play a male is trying to dominate a female – where do your sympathies lie? What kind of character is Titania – or isn't it helpful to view her in this 'mortal' way?

2 Cut it out (in pairs)

Shakespeare's plays are often cut for performance (that is, shortened by leaving some lines or speeches out). Read aloud/act out this passage, and then do it again leaving out lines 123–37. What difference does leaving out these lines make?

3 Love as magic (in groups of four to six)

On page 37, Oberon introduces the flower whose juice on a sleepers' eyelids makes them 'madly dote' on the first person they see when they awake. The idea of love potions is ancient, but even today the connection is often made between love and magic. Discuss why this might be.

4 Love is the drug (in groups of four to six)

The fairies' perception of the world is different from that of the mortals. It could be presented as a drug-induced state with the fairies intoxicated or 'high'. The flower could also act as a kind of hallucinogen which changes people's perception of others. Does this interpretation work? It would certainly be a way in for a modern audience.

---

henchman page
votress member of religious order,
  worshipper
chide argue, criticise

OBERON Do you amend it, then: it lies in you.
        Why should Titania cross her Oberon?
        I do but beg a little changeling boy   120
        To be my henchman.
TITANIA   Set your heart at rest.
        The fairy land buys not the child of me.
        His mother was a votress of my order,
        And in the spicèd Indian air by night
        Full often hath she gossiped by my side,   125
        And sat with me on Neptune's yellow sands
        Marking th'embarkèd traders on the flood,
        When we have laughed to see the sails conceive
        And grow big-bellied with the wanton wind;
        Which she, with pretty and with swimming gait   130
        Following (her womb then rich with my young squire),
        Would imitate, and sail upon the land
        To fetch me trifles, and return again
        As from a voyage, rich with merchandise.
        But she, being mortal, of that boy did die,   135
        And for her sake do I rear up her boy;
        And for her sake I will not part with him.
OBERON How long within this wood intend you stay?
TITANIA Perchance till after Theseus' wedding day.
        If you will patiently dance in our round,   140
        And see our moonlight revels, go with us:
        If not, shun me, and I will spare your haunts.
OBERON Give me that boy, and I will go with thee.
TITANIA Not for thy fairy kingdom! Fairies, away.
        We shall chide downright if I longer stay.   145
                 Exeunt [Titania and her train]
OBERON Well, go thy way. Thou shalt not from this grove
        Till I torment thee for this injury.

Oberon tells Puck to fetch him 'love-in-idleness' (a flower touched by Cupid's arrow). When the juice of the flower is put on the eyelids of the sleeping it makes them fall in love with whatever they see when they awake.

Oberon and Puck (Renaissance Theatre Company, 1990).

spheres orbits
Cupid's fiery shaft Cupid's arrow which was supposed to make the person that it hit fall in love

bolt arrow
leviathan whale

My gentle Puck, come hither. Thou rememberest
Since once I sat upon a promontory,
And heard a mermaid on a dolphin's back   150
Uttering such dulcet and harmonious breath
That the rude sea grew civil at her song,
And certain stars shot madly from their spheres
To hear the sea-maid's music?

PUCK   I remember.

OBERON That very time I saw (but thou couldst not)   155
Flying between the cold moon and the earth
Cupid all armed: a certain aim he took
At a fair vestal thronèd by the west,
And loosed his loveshaft smartly from his bow
As it should pierce a hundred thousand hearts;   160
But I might see young Cupid's fiery shaft
Quenched in the chaste beams of the watery moon;
And the imperial votress passèd on
In maiden meditation, fancy-free.
Yet marked I where the bolt of Cupid fell: 165
It fell upon a little western flower,
Before, milk-white; now purple with love's wound:
And maidens call it 'love-in-idleness'.
Fetch me that flower, the herb I showed thee once;
The juice of it on sleeping eyelids laid   170
Will make or man or woman madly dote
Upon the next live creature that it sees.
Fetch me this herb, and be thou here again
Ere the leviathan can swim a league.

PUCK I'll put a girdle round about the earth   175
In forty minutes!   [*Exit*]

Oberon plans to use the flower's juice on Titania, then makes himself invisible as Demetrius and Helena enter, arguing.

---

1 Oberon's revenge (in pairs)

Read aloud Oberon's plan (lines 176–85) and then consider whether he is fair in doing this.

2 The argument (1) (in pairs)

The scene in lines 188–213 is very enjoyable to act out, but read it aloud first. Shakespeare was very fond of word-play (especially in his early comedies), and this is a good example. Look at the patterns of words, and identify some of the different kinds of word-play here. Read it again, emphasising this word-play.

3 The argument (2) (in pairs)

Read through the argument again, looking at what the characters are feeling – like Titania and Oberon, they are upset and angry. The image of being Demetrius' dog that Helena uses is hardly very pleasant. Try reading it to emphasise these feelings.

4 The argument (3) (in pairs)

Now get up and act out the argument, perhaps in different ways, stressing the feelings, or the silliness of it all.

5 The fairy and mortal worlds (in groups of four to six)

Oberon is 'invisible' to the mortals. This – and what has gone before – suggest the extent of his powers. Discuss what sort of relationship there is between the worlds of the mortals and of the fairies.

---

wood mad, insane while he is in a
real wood. Elizabethans were fond
of word-play and puns, as this page
shows
adamant hard stone, diamond

OBERON   Having once this juice
                I'll watch Titania when she is asleep,
                And drop the liquor of it in her eyes:
                The next thing then she, waking, looks upon –
                Be it on lion, bear, or wolf, or bull,   180
                On meddling monkey, or on busy ape –
                She shall pursue it with the soul of love.
                And ere I take this charm from off her sight
                (As I can take it with another herb)
                I'll make her render up her page to me.   185
                But who comes here? I am invisible,
                And I will overhear their conference.

                Enter DEMETRIUS, HELENA *following him*

DEMETRIUS I love thee not, therefore pursue me not.
                Where is Lysander, and fair Hermia?
                The one I'll slay, the other slayeth me.   190
                Thou told'st me they were stol'n unto this wood,
                And here am I, and wood within this wood
                Because I cannot meet my Hermia.
                Hence, get thee gone, and follow me no more.
HELENA You draw me, you hard-hearted adamant!   195
                But yet you draw not iron, for my heart
                Is true as steel. Leave you your power to draw,
                And I shall have no power to follow you.
DEMETRIUS Do I entice you? Do I speak you fair?
                Or rather do I not in plainest truth   200
                Tell you I do not, nor I cannot love you?
HELENA And even for that do I love you the more.
                I am your spaniel; and, Demetrius,
                The more you beat me I will fawn on you.
                Use me but as your spaniel: spurn me, strike me,   205
                Neglect me, lose me; only give me leave,
                Unworthy as I am, to follow you.
                What worser place can I beg in your love
                (And yet a place of high respect with me)
                Than to be usèd as you use your dog?   210
DEMETRIUS Tempt not too much the hatred of my spirit;
                For I am sick when I do look on thee.
HELENA And I am sick when I look not on you.

Helena continues to woo Demetrius, who argues with her and eventually runs off.

---

1 Reclaim the night (in groups of four to six)

Read Demetrius' first speech (lines 214–19), and think carefully about the implications of his threat. Women are more often attacked at night, and in places like a wood. The problems of women's safety at night were obviously real in Shakespeare's day. Discuss whether there are solutions.

2 Role reversal? (in groups of four to six)

Re-read lines 241–2. Decide whether you think this is true or not. Helena points out that it reverses the usual stories (in these stories Apollo chased Daphne, the griffin pursued the dove and the tiger the deer ('hind')). Do you consider Helena's actions unnatural? (you can compare her with other young women you know).

3 Anything Shakespeare can do, I can do

Helena's couplet at the end (the two rhyming lines 243–4) sums up her feelings. Write a couplet for Demetrius to say to Helena just before he leaves that sum up *his* feelings.

4 Oberon – the master? (in groups of four to six)

In his two speeches on page 43 Oberon shows his power over the lives of both mortals and fairies. There is a sense in which the male characters dominate the play (Theseus in Athens, Oberon in the wood). Perhaps this is simply Shakespeare reflecting the prejudices (and realities?) of his time. Or perhaps it is the fact that they have positions of great power (duke, king). Discuss whether this male domination makes any difference to your responses to the characters or to the play.

---

impeach call into question
desert lonely, deserted
brakes undergrowth, thicket

griffin beast, half eagle, half lion
bootless useless

DEMETRIUS You do impeach your modesty too much,
　　　　　To leave the city and commit yourself　　　　　215
　　　　　Into the hands of one that loves you not;
　　　　　To trust the opportunity of night,
　　　　　And the ill counsel of a desert place,
　　　　　With the rich worth of your virginity.
HELENA Your virtue is my privilege: for that　　　　　220
　　　　　It is not night when I do see your face,
　　　　　Therefore I think I am not in the night;
　　　　　Nor doth this wood lack worlds of company,
　　　　　For you, in my respect, are all the world.
　　　　　Then how can it be said I am alone　　　　　225
　　　　　When all the world is here to look on me?
DEMETRIUS I'll run from thee and hide me in the brakes,
　　　　　And leave thee to the mercy of wild beasts.
HELENA The wildest hath not such a heart as you.
　　　　　Run when you will: the story shall be changed;　　　　　230
　　　　　Apollo flies, and Daphne holds the chase,
　　　　　The dove pursues the griffin, the mild hind
　　　　　Makes speed to catch the tiger – bootless speed,
　　　　　When cowardice pursues, and valour flies!
DEMETRIUS I will not stay thy questions. Let me go;　　　　　235
　　　　　Or if thou follow me, do not believe
　　　　　But I shall do thee mischief in the wood.
HELENA Ay, in the temple, in the town, the field,
　　　　　You do me mischief. Fie, Demetrius,
　　　　　Your wrongs do set a scandal on my sex!　　　　　240
　　　　　We cannot fight for love, as men may do;
　　　　　We should be wooed, and were not made to woo.
　　　　　　　　　　　　　　　　[*Exit Demetrius*]
　　　　　I'll follow thee, and make a heaven of hell,
　　　　　To die upon the hand I love so well.　　　　　*Exit*

Oberon vows to help Helena. Puck returns with the flower. Oberon will use it on Titania when she is asleep. He tells Puck to use it on Demetrius when Helena is near.

Oberon and Puck (Royal Exchange Theatre, 1988).

ere before
weed cloth

OBERON Fare thee well, nymph. Ere he do leave this grove   245
        Thou shalt fly him, and he shall seek thy love.

Enter PUCK

        Hast thou the flower there? Welcome, wanderer.
PUCK Ay, there it is.
OBERON   I pray thee give it me.
        I know a bank where the wild thyme blows,
        Where oxlips and the nodding violet grows,   250
        Quite overcanopied with luscious woodbine,
        With sweet musk-roses, and with eglantine:
        There sleeps Titania sometime of the night,
        Lulled in these flowers with dances and delight;
        And there the snake throws her enamelled skin,   255
        Weed wide enough to wrap a fairy in;
        And with the juice of this I'll streak her eyes,
        And make her full of hateful fantasies.
        Take thou some of it, and seek through this grove:
        A sweet Athenian lady is in love   260
        With a disdainful youth; anoint his eyes,
        But do it when the next thing he espies
        May be the lady. Thou shalt know the man
        By the Athenian garments he hath on.
        Effect it with some care, that he may prove   265
        More fond on her than she upon her love.
        And look thou meet me ere the first cock crow.
PUCK Fear not, my lord; your servant shall do so.
                                        Exeunt

Titania is sung to sleep by her fairies.

---

1 Photographic record (in groups of five to six)

Look at the photograph on page 24. Think about the variety of ways in which you could present the fairies here (body position, facial expression). Then create a variety of tableaux ('frozen moments') and photograph them. If you have the means, you could experiment with make-up and costumes.

2 Say it with newts (in groups of six)

This passage (lines 1–32) has a chorus, where a group read or sing together. With four people as the chorus, read the whole passage. Like the words in a lot of songs, if it's just read out, it can sound odd. Try to compose a song to these words, then perform it as a group.

---

roundel a dance in a circle
reremice bats
philomel nightingale

ACT 2 SCENE 2
The wood

Enter TITANIA, Queen of Fairies, with her train

TITANIA Come, now a roundel and a fairy song,
Then for the third part of a minute, hence –
Some to kill cankers in the musk-rose buds,
Some war with reremice for their leathern wings
To make my small elves coats, and some keep back   5
The clamorous owl that nightly hoots and wonders
At our quaint spirits. Sing me now asleep;
Then to your offices, and let me rest.
Fairies sing.

[FIRST FAIRY] You spotted snakes with double tongue,
Thorny hedgehogs, be not seen.   10
Newts and blindworms, do no wrong,
Come not near our Fairy Queen.
[CHORUS] Philomel with melody
Sing in our sweet lullaby,
Lulla, lulla, lullaby; lulla, lulla, lullaby.   15
Never harm
Nor spell nor charm
Come our lovely lady nigh.
So good night, with lullaby.
FIRST FAIRY Weaving spiders, come not here;   20
Hence, you longlegged spinners, hence!
Beetles black approach not near;
Worm nor snail, do no offence.
[CHORUS] Philomel with melody
Sing in our sweet lullaby,   25
Lulla, lulla, lullaby; lulla, lulla, lullaby.
Never harm
Nor spell nor charm
Come our lovely lady nigh.
So good night, with lullaby.   *Titania sleeps.*   30
SECOND FAIRY
Hence, away! Now all is well;
One aloof stand sentinel!   [*Exeunt Fairies*]

Oberon puts the flower's juice on Titania's eyes with a charm that she will wake 'when some vile thing is near'. Lysander and Hermia enter, lost, and prepare to sleep.

1 Vile thing, you make my heart sing (in groups of three)

Discuss Oberon's speech (lines 33–40) and the idea of wanting your partner to be in love with an animal.

2 Contrast the kinds of love (in groups of three)

Taking parts, read this passage aloud, and then talk about the different kinds of love in each part (Oberon's speech versus Lysander and Hermia's).

3 Young love

Write the thoughts and feelings of Hermia (and, separately, Lysander) as they drift off to sleep, looking back on the events of the play. You can try writing in rhyming couplets as Shakespeare does here.

4 Just a thought

Line 67 is ironic (since Lysander's love alters in a few minutes, thanks to Puck putting the flower's juice on his eyes instead of Demetrius'). Look out for other ironies in what people say or do.

5 Theatres in Shakespeare's day (in groups of three)

Look at the drawing on page 48: it is of the Swan Theatre in 1596 (*A Midsummer Night's Dream* was probably written in 1595 or 1596). Talk about a production of the play in this theatre, and what it would have been like.

---

ounce lynx
pard leopard

troth truth
much beshrew a curse upon

Enter OBERON; [*he squeezes the juice on Titania's eyes*]

OBERON What thou seest when thou dost wake,
Do it for thy true love take;
Love and languish for his sake.   35
Be it ounce or cat or bear,
Pard, or boar with bristled hair
In thy eye that shall appear
When thou wak'st, it is thy dear.
Wake when some vile thing is near!   [*Exit*]   40

Enter LYSANDER *and* HERMIA

LYSANDER Fair love, you faint with wandering in the wood,
And, to speak truth, I have forgot our way.
We'll rest us, Hermia, if you think it good,
And tarry for the comfort of the day.
HERMIA Be it so, Lysander; find you out a bed,   45
For I upon this bank will rest my head.
LYSANDER One turf shall serve as pillow for us both;
One heart, one bed, two bosoms, and one troth.
HERMIA Nay, good Lysander, for my sake, my dear,
Lie further off yet; do not lie so near.   50
LYSANDER O take the sense, sweet, of my innocence!
Love takes the meaning in love's conference;
I mean that my heart unto yours is knit,
So that but one heart we can make of it:
Two bosoms interchainèd with an oath,   55
So then two bosoms and a single troth.
Then by your side no bed-room me deny,
For lying so, Hermia, I do not lie.
HERMIA Lysander riddles very prettily.
Now much beshrew my manners and my pride   60
If Hermia meant to say Lysander lied.
But, gentle friend, for love and courtesy
Lie further off, in human modesty;
Such separation as may well be said
Becomes a virtuous bachelor and a maid,   65
So far be distant, and good night, sweet friend;
Thy love ne'er alter till thy sweet life end!

Hermia and Lysander sleep, and Puck mistakenly puts the juice in Lysander's eyes. Demetrius enters chased by Helena. Demetrius runs off into the wood on his own.

The Swan Playhouse, 1596.

approve put to the proof
weeds clothes

churl heartless rogue
darkling sad, downcast

LYSANDER Amen, amen, to that fair prayer say I,
       And then end life when I end loyalty!
       Here is my bed; sleep give thee all his rest.   70
HERMIA With half that wish the wisher's eyes be pressed.
                 They sleep.

                Enter PUCK

PUCK   Through the forest have I gone,
          But Athenian found I none
          On whose eyes I might approve
          This flower's force in stirring love.   75
          Night and silence – Who is here?
          Weeds of Athens he doth wear:
          This is he my master said
          Despisèd the Athenian maid;
          And here the maiden, sleeping sound   80
          On the dank and dirty ground.
          Pretty soul, she durst not lie
          Near this lack-love, this kill-courtesy.
          Churl, upon thy eyes I throw
          All the power this charm doth owe.   85
          [*He squeezes the juice on Lysander's eyes.*]
          When thou wak'st let love forbid
          Sleep his seat on thy eyelid.
          So, awake when I am gone;
          For I must now to Oberon.   *Exit*

      Enter DEMETRIUS *and* HELENA, *running*

HELENA Stay, though thou kill me, sweet Demetrius!   90
DEMETRIUS I charge thee, hence, and do not haunt me thus.
HELENA O wilt thou darkling leave me? Do not so!
DEMETRIUS Stay, on thy peril; I alone will go.   *Exit*

*Helena stops to rest, sees Lysander, and wakes him. He wakes up,
and immediately falls in love with Helena because of the flower's magic.*

---

1 Shall I compare me to a bear? (in groups of three)

Read through Helena's speech about her own appearance (lines
94–108). Why might she feel this way about herself?

2 Lysander – or not Lysander? (in groups of three)

'Lysander gets taken over when he's under the influence of magic;
that's where character tends to disappear. It brings out all this raw
passion.' James Larkin, Lysander in the Renaissance
Theatre Company production.

Try various ways of presenting a transformed Lysander. Share
ideas with other groups, and discuss the results and implications.

3 What to make of him (in groups of three)

We know that Lysander's 'love' is just magic, but for Helena the
Athenian world of conventions and normality must seem far away.
Talk about what Helena must think of Lysander's sudden transfor-
mation.

4 The dance of the lovers – who loves whom?

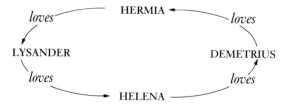

---

fond foolish
sphery star-like
transparent honest, open

HELENA   O, I am out of breath in this fond chase!
      The more my prayer, the lesser is my grace.   95
      Happy is Hermia, wheresoe'er she lies,
      For she hath blessèd and attractive eyes.
      How came her eyes so bright? Not with salt tears –
      If so, my eyes are oftener washed than hers.
      No, no, I am as ugly as a bear,   100
      For beasts that meet me run away for fear.
      Therefore no marvel though Demetrius
      Do as a monster fly my presence thus.
      What wicked and dissembling glass of mine
      Made me compare with Hermia's sphery eyne?   105
      But who is here? – Lysander, on the ground?
      Dead, or asleep? I see no blood, no wound.
      Lysander, if you live, good sir, awake!
LYSANDER [*Waking.*]
      And run through fire I will for thy sweet sake!
      Transparent Helena, nature shows art   110
      That through thy bosom makes me see thy heart.
      Where is Demetrius? O, how fit a word
      Is that vile name to perish on my sword!
HELENA   Do not say so, Lysander, say not so.
      What though he love your Hermia? Lord, what though?   115
      Yet Hermia still loves you; then be content.
LYSANDER   Content with Hermia? No; I do repent
      The tedious minutes I with her have spent.
      Not Hermia, but Helena I love.
      Who will not change a raven for a dove?   120
      The will of man is by his reason swayed,
      And reason says you are the worthier maid.
      Things growing are not ripe until their season;
      So I, being young, till now ripe not to reason.
      And touching now the point of human skill,   125
      Reason becomes the marshal to my will.
      And leads me to your eyes, where I o'erlook
      Love's stories written in love's richest book.

Helena thinks Lysander is making fun of her, and runs off. He follows, leaving Hermia behind. Hermia awakes from a nightmare, finds herself alone, and goes to find Lysander.

1 What means this dream? (in groups of three)

Talk together about what Hermia's dream might mean.

2 Babes in a wood (in groups of three)

There are three characters, three moods, and three different 'dreams' of what is happening here. None of the three characters really understands what is going on. Each choose a character and read their speech aloud, and describe the character's mood and 'dream' of what is happening.

3 Men and women (in groups of three)

Compare the two women's speeches opposite, and see if there are any similarities. Then contrast them with Lysander's. If you have found differences between the men and women's speeches here, share them with the whole class and discuss the implications.

4 Absolute confusion? (in groups of three)

Look at the note on page 50 about the 'dance' of the lovers – things couldn't get worse. Then find as many negative/upsetting images as you can on this page. Read aloud just those images. Perhaps a midsummer night's dream is becoming a nightmare.

5 'Seemed Athens as a paradise to me' (in groups of three)

Hermia entered the wood with high hopes. Compare the world she finds herself in now (the wood, the night, the magic) with the one she left behind.

---

surfeit surplus, too much
heresy false religious belief

HELENA Wherefore was I to this keen mockery born?
          When at your hands did I deserve this scorn?   130
          Is't not enough, is't not enough, young man,
          That I did never, no, nor never can
          Deserve a sweet look from Demetrius' eye
          But you must flout my insufficiency?
          Good troth, you do me wrong, good sooth, you do,   135
          In such disdainful manner me to woo!
          But fare you well: perforce I must confess
          I thought you lord of more true gentleness.
          O, that a lady of one man refused
          Should of another therefore be abused!   *Exit* 140
LYSANDER She sees not Hermia. Hermia, sleep thou there,
          And never mayst thou come Lysander near.
          For, as a surfeit of the sweetest things
          The deepest loathing to the stomach brings,
          Or as the heresies that men do leave   145
          Are hated most of those they did deceive,
          So thou, my surfeit and my heresy,
          Of all be hated, but the most of me!
          And, all my powers, address your love and might
          To honour Helen, and to be her knight.   *Exit* 150
HERMIA [*Waking.*]
          Help me, Lysander, help me! Do thy best
          To pluck this crawling serpent from my breast!
          Ay me, for pity! What a dream was here!
          Lysander, look how I do quake with fear –
          Methought a serpent ate my heart away,   155
          And you sat smiling at his cruel prey.
          Lysander! What, removed? Lysander, lord!
          What, out of hearing? Gone? No sound, no word?
          Alack, where are you? Speak and if you hear.
          Speak, of all loves! I swoon almost with fear.   160
          No? Then I well perceive you are not nigh.
          Either death or you I'll find immediately.   *Exit*

A Midsummer Night's Dream

The Mechanicals (Renaissance Theatre Company, 1990).

In the wood near the sleeping Titania, the Mechanicals begin their rehearsal with Bottom suggesting changes in the play to make it less frightening.

1 Bottom's play (in groups of six)

Of course it is Quince's play, but Bottom certainly has ideas for it. Look at Bottom's suggestions on pages 57 and 59, reading them aloud, and then talking about them (and what they tell us about Bottom himself). Improvise the additions and changes suggested here (with Quince doing the Prologue, Snug playing the lion, Starveling the moon, and Snout the wall).

2 What do they think of Bottom? (in groups of six)

Each person take on the role of one of the Mechanicals. Explain what your character thinks of Bottom from what he says and does on pages 57 and 59. Include what Bottom thinks of himself. Then talk about what you think about Bottom and compare it with the Mechanicals' view.

3 Rehearsal within a play (in groups of six)

Not only is there a play within *A Midsummer Night's Dream*, there are even rehearsals. Perhaps Shakespeare was mocking amateur dramatics because he was in one of the very first professional theatre companies in England. What other reasons might there be?

4 Watch your language (in groups of two to three)

The Mechanicals don't just speak in prose, they use a less formal, less literary kind of language. Write a short scene of modern workers rehearsing (feel free to exaggerate a bit). Write a short scene with modern middle-class, or literary and artistic lovers (again, exaggerate if you want). Compare the kind of language each group uses.

---

brake thicket
bully adjective that implies respect and admiration

by'r lakin by our lady (an exclamation)

ACT 3 SCENE I
The wood

Enter the Clowns [, BOTTOM, QUINCE, SNOUT, STARVELING, SNUG and FLUTE. TITANIA remains on stage, asleep]

BOTTOM Are we all met?

QUINCE Pat, pat; and here's a marvellous convenient place for our rehearsal. This green plot shall be our stage, this hawthorn brake our tiring-house, and we will do it in action as we will do it before the Duke.   5

BOTTOM Peter Quince!

QUINCE What sayest thou, bully Bottom?

BOTTOM There are things in this comedy of Pyramus and Thisbe that will never please. First, Pyramus must draw a sword to kill himself, which the ladies cannot abide. How answer you that?   10

SNOUT By'r lakin, a parlous fear!

STARVELING I believe we must leave the killing out, when all is done.

BOTTOM Not a whit; I have a device to make all well. Write me a prologue, and let the prologue seem to say we will do no harm with our swords, and that Pyramus is not killed indeed; and for the more   15
better assurance, tell them that I, Pyramus, am not Pyramus, but Bottom the weaver: this will put them out of fear.

QUINCE Well, we will have such a prologue; and it shall be written in eight and six.

BOTTOM No, make it two more: let it be written in eight and eight.   20

SNOUT Will not the ladies be afeard of the lion?

STARVELING I fear it, I promise you.

BOTTOM Masters, you ought to consider with yourself, to bring in (God shield us!) a lion among ladies is a most dreadful thing; for there is not a more fearful wildfowl than your lion living; and we ought   25
to look to't.

SNOUT Therefore another prologue must tell he is not a lion.

BOTTOM Nay, you must name his name, and half his face must be seen through the lion's neck, and he himself must speak through, saying thus, or to the same defect: 'Ladies', or 'Fair ladies, I would wish   30
you', or 'I would request you', or 'I would entreat you, not to fear, not to tremble: my life for yours. If you think I come hither as a lion, it were pity of my life. No, I am no such thing; I am a man,

The Mechanicals discuss how to show moonlight and the wall in the play, and decide they must have an actor represent each.

The Mechanicals (Royal Shakespeare Company, 1977).

as other men are' – and there indeed let him name his name, and
tell them plainly he is Snug the joiner.   35

QUINCE Well, it shall be so. But there is two hard things: that is, to
bring the moonlight into a chamber; for, you know, Pyramus and
Thisbe meet by moonlight.

SNUG Doth the moon shine that night we play our play?

BOTTOM A calendar, a calendar! Look in the almanac – find out   40
moonshine, find out moonshine!

QUINCE Yes, it doth shine that night.

BOTTOM Why, then may you leave a casement of the great chamber
window, where we play, open, and the moon may shine in at the
casement.   45

QUINCE Ay; or else one must come in with a bush of thorns and a
lantern, and say he comes to disfigure, or to present the person of
Moonshine. Then there is another thing: we must have a wall in
the great chamber; for Pyramus and Thisbe, says the story, did talk
through the chink of a wall.   50

SNOUT You can never bring in a wall. What say you, Bottom?

BOTTOM Some man or other must present Wall; and let him have some
plaster, or some loam, or some rough-cast about him to signify Wall;
or let him hold his fingers thus, and through that cranny shall
Pyramus and Thisbe whisper.   55

QUINCE If that may be, then all is well. Come, sit down every mother's
son, and rehearse your parts. Pyramus, you begin. When you have
spoken your speech, enter into that brake, and so everyone
according to his cue.

*Puck enters and watches as the Mechanicals begin to rehearse, going off
with Bottom when he goes off-stage. After getting his lines muddled,
Flute gives Bottom his cue to reappear.*

1 Invisible (in groups of six to seven)

Puck is invisible here (in that the Mechanicals can't see him although
the audience can). Think how you might act this as the Mechanicals
continue their rehearsal.

2 Acting badly is good (in groups of six to seven)

Talk about the complications of acting characters who are in the
process of attempting to act but failing. Consider how the timing of
what you say might help bring out the Mechanicals' bad acting.

3 The transformation (1) (in groups of six to seven)

Rehearse and act out the passages on pages 61 and 63. The farce of
the rehearsal turns into the farce of Bottom being an ass, but it offers
lots of opportunity for knockabout comedy. You can video the scene,
using lots of close-ups and cuts, or perform it directly to the rest of
the class.

4 The transformation (2) (in groups of six to seven)

There are many myths about people being transformed into animals,
including asses. Of course, Bottom is an ass (fool) already. Some
people have seen a darker side to this, associating the ass with sexual
prowess. Others see it as a mockery of romance. Compare the
photographs on pages 54–5 and 66 – which do you prefer?

---

hempen homespuns they are
  dressed in rough, homemade
  clothes
eke also

Enter PUCK

PUCK What hempen homespuns have we swaggering here   60
   So near the cradle of the Fairy Queen?
   What, a play toward? I'll be an auditor,
   An actor too perhaps, if I see cause.
QUINCE Speak, Pyramus! Thisbe, stand forth!
BOTTOM (*as Pyramus*)
   Thisbe, the flowers of odious savours sweet –   65
QUINCE Odours – 'odorous'!
BOTTOM (*as Pyramus*)   …odours savours sweet.
   So hath thy breath, my dearest Thisbe dear.
   But hark, a voice! Stay thou but here awhile,
   And by and by I will to thee appear.   *Exit* 70
PUCK A stranger Pyramus than e'er played here.   [*Exit*]
FLUTE Must I speak now?
QUINCE Ay, marry must you; for you must understand he goes but to
 see a noise that he heard, and is to come again.
FLUTE (*as Thisbe*)
   Most radiant Pyramus, most lilywhite of hue,   75
    Of colour like the red rose on triumphant briar,
   Most brisky juvenal, and eke most lovely Jew,
    As true as truest horse that yet would never tire,
   I'll meet thee, Pyramus, at Ninny's tomb –
QUINCE 'Ninus' tomb', man! – Why, you must not speak that yet; that   80
 you answer to Pyramus. You speak all your part at once, cues and
 all. Pyramus, enter – your cue is past. It is 'never tire'.
FLUTE O –
  (*as Thisbe*)
  As true as truest horse, that yet would never tire.

Bottom re-enters with an ass's head (because of Puck's magic), and everyone runs off. Bottom thinks they are teasing him.

The Mechanicals, from an eighteenth-century book.

ousel blackbird
cock male bird

Enter PUCK, *and* BOTTOM *with the ass head on*

BOTTOM (*as Pyramus*)
      If I were fair, fair Thisbe, I were only thine.   85
QUINCE O monstrous! O strange! We are haunted! Pray, masters, fly,
    masters! Help!
                    Exeunt Quince, Snug, Flute, Snout and Starveling
PUCK   I'll follow you: I'll lead you about a round,
      Through bog, through bush, through brake, through briar;
      Sometime a horse I'll be, sometime a hound,   90
        A hog, a headless bear, sometime a fire,
      And neigh, and bark, and grunt, and roar, and burn,
      Like horse, hound, hog, bear, fire at every turn.   *Exit*
BOTTOM Why do they run away? This is a knavery of them to make
    me afeard.   95

Enter SNOUT

SNOUT O Bottom, thou art changed. What do I see on thee?
BOTTOM What do you see? You see an ass head of your own, do you?
                                  [*Exit Snout*]

Enter QUINCE

QUINCE Bless thee, Bottom, bless thee! Thou art translated!   *Exit*
BOTTOM I see their knavery. This is to make an ass of me, to fright
    me, if they could; but I will not stir from this place, do what they   100
    can. I will walk up and down here, and will sing, that they shall
    hear I am not afraid.
    [*Sings.*] The ousel cock so black of hue,
         With orange-tawny bill,
      The throstle with his note so true,   105
         The wren with little quill –

Bottom's song wakes Titania who instantly falls in love with him,
and vows to keep him with her.

---

1 'What angel wakes me from my flowery bed?' (in pairs)

Line 107 is one of Shakespeare's most famous lines, even though it is ironic. Read through the opposite page aloud, thinking about how you could act it – but don't just yet . . .

2 Transformations (in pairs)

Think carefully about the nature of the transformations here. Bottom's behaviour and speech might change (as his head has done) to become more like a real ass, or he might stay the same 'bully Bottom'. Certainly the transformed Titania is behaving differently from when she confronted Oberon. Experiment with tone, movement and manner for both characters. Then act out the whole passage.

3 'Reason and love keep little company together nowadays' (in pairs)

What has the relationship between reason and love been in the play so far? Identify those characters who are being reasonable, and those that are dominated by their emotions, particularly love.

4 Fairy world and mortal world (in groups of four to six)

This is the only meeting of the fairy and the mortal worlds in the play, in that the mortals can see and talk to the fairies. On the other hand, both characters have been transformed (in a sense they are having visions or dreams). Discuss what sort of relationship the two have on pages 65 and 67, and look at the photograph on page 66 as well.

---

set his wit to set his wits against,
  argue with
give . . . the lie contradict, call a
  liar
gleek joke

TITANIA [*Waking.*] What angel wakes me from my flowery bed?

BOTTOM [*Sings.*]
> The finch, the sparrow, and the lark,
>> The plainsong cuckoo grey,
>> Whose note full many a man doth mark 110
>> And dares not answer nay –

for indeed, who would set his wit to so foolish a bird? Who would give a bird the lie, though he cry 'cuckoo' never so?

TITANIA I pray thee, gentle mortal, sing again;
> Mine ear is much enamoured of thy note. 115
> So is mine eye enthrallèd to thy shape,
> And thy fair virtue's force perforce doth move me
> On the first view to say, to swear, I love thee.

BOTTOM Methinks, mistress, you should have little reason for that. And yet, to say the truth, reason and love keep little company together 120 nowadays; the more the pity that some honest neighbours will not make them friends. Nay, I can gleek upon occasion.

TITANIA Thou art as wise as thou art beautiful.

BOTTOM Not so neither; but if I had wit enough to get out of this wood, I have enough to serve mine own turn. 125

TITANIA Out of this wood do not desire to go:
> Thou shalt remain here, whether thou wilt or no.
> I am a spirit of no common rate;
> The summer still doth tend upon my state,
> And I do love thee. Therefore go with me. 130
> I'll give thee fairies to attend on thee,
> And they shall fetch thee jewels from the deep,
> And sing, while thou on pressèd flowers dost sleep;
> And I will purge thy mortal grossness so
> That thou shalt like an airy spirit go. 135
> Peaseblossom, Cobweb, Moth, and Mustardseed!

Enter four Fairies.

PEASEBLOSSOM Ready.
COBWEB And I.
MOTH And I.
MUSTARDSEED And I. 140

Titania asks her fairies to look after Bottom. He asks their names.
Bottom is then led to Titania's bower.

Bottom, Titania and the fairies (Royal Shakespeare Company, 1962).

ALL Where shall we go?
TITANIA Be kind and courteous to this gentleman:
          Hop in his walks and gambol in his eyes;
          Feed him with apricocks and dewberries,
          With purple grapes, green figs, and mulberries;   145
          The honey-bags steal from the humble-bees,
          And for night-tapers crop their waxen thighs,
          And light them at the fiery glow-worms' eyes
          To have my love to bed, and to arise;
          And pluck the wings from painted butterflies   150
          To fan the moonbeams from his sleeping eyes.
          Nod to him, elves, and do him courtesies.
PEASEBLOSSOM Hail, mortal!
COBWEB Hail!
MOTH Hail!   155
MUSTARDSEED Hail!
BOTTOM I cry your worships mercy, heartily. I beseech your worship's
          name.
COBWEB Cobweb.
BOTTOM I shall desire you of more acquaintance, good Master Cobweb;   160
          if I cut my finger I shall make bold with you. Your name, honest
          gentleman?
PEASEBLOSSOM Peaseblossom.
BOTTOM I pray you commend me to Mistress Squash, your mother,
          and to Master Peascod, your father. Good Master Peaseblossom,   165
          I shall desire you of more acquaintance, too. – Your name, I
          beseech you, sir?
MUSTARDSEED Mustardseed.
BOTTOM Good Master Mustardseed, I know your patience well. That
          same cowardly, giant-like ox-beef hath devoured many a gentleman   170
          of your house. I promise you, your kindred hath made my eyes
          water ere now. I desire you of more acquaintance, good Master
          Mustardseed.
TITANIA Come, wait upon him. Lead him to my bower.
          The moon methinks looks with a watery eye,   175
          And when she weeps, weeps every little flower,
          Lamenting some enforcèd chastity.
          Tie up my lover's tongue; bring him silently.
                                                        Exeunt

Oberon and Puck arrive, and Puck explains what has happened with Titania and Bottom.

---

1 Puck's view of the Mechanicals (in groups of four to six)

One person reads Puck's speech (lines 6–34), with the others miming some of the Mechanicals' behaviour. Find all the words and images he uses about the Mechanicals, and then talk about Puck's view of them (for example, he calls Bottom 'the shallowest thick-skin of that barren sort').

2 Imagine (in groups of four to six)

Remind yourselves of what happened earlier (see pages 61 and 63), and compare it with the description here. Then consider which you find most effective. Consider why Shakespeare chose to relate what we have just seen in this way.

3 Just a detail (in groups of two to three)

Look at lines 21–3 – this is an extended comparison of the Mechanicals and the birds scattering. Compose some extended comparisons yourself, trying to pick ones that capture the Mechanicals' confusion. Try to write first in prose, and then in couplets. Read them aloud to each other and decide which was easier to write.

---

patches clowns
nole head

ACT 3   SCENE 2
The wood

Enter OBERON, King of Fairies

OBERON I wonder if Titania be awaked;
      Then what it was that next came in her eye,
      Which she must dote on, in extremity.

Enter PUCK

      Here comes my messenger. How now, mad spirit?
      What night-rule now about this haunted grove? 5
PUCK My mistress with a monster is in love.
      Near to her close and consecrated bower,
      While she was in her dull and sleeping hour,
      A crew of patches, rude mechanicals,
      That work for bread upon Athenian stalls, 10
      Were met together to rehearse a play
      Intended for great Theseus' nuptial day.
      The shallowest thick-skin of that barren sort,
      Who Pyramus presented, in their sport
      Forsook his scene and entered in a brake, 15
      When I did him at this advantage take:
      An ass's nole I fixèd on his head.
      Anon his Thisbe must be answerèd,
      And forth my mimic comes. When they him spy –
      As wild geese that the creeping fowler eye, 20
      Or russet-pated choughs, many in sort,
      Rising and cawing at the gun's report,
      Sever themselves and madly sweep the sky –
      So at his sight away his fellows fly,
      And at our stamp here o'er and o'er one falls; 25
      He 'Murder!' cries, and help from Athens calls.
      Their sense thus weak, lost with their fears thus strong,
      Made senseless things begin to do them wrong,
      For briars and thorns at their apparel snatch,
      Some sleeves, some hats; from yielders all things catch. 30

Oberon is pleased, and Puck says he has also dealt with the 'Athenian'.
Demetrius enters, trying to court Hermia who accuses him of having
murdered Lysander.

1 Two worlds, two views (in groups of four)

Split into two pairs. One read and rehearse the Oberon/Puck
conversation on page 71 (lines 35–42) and page 73 (lines 88–101),
and the other the argument between Demetrius and Hermia (lines
43–87). Then put them together. Afterwards consider what difference it makes having them together, and how the two worlds differ.

2 Darkness and confusion (in pairs)

Even Puck makes mistakes, and the feelings of Hermia and Demetrius are now out in the open. Look at their argument on page 71 and
find the words and images that best bring out their mood. Then just
read those words and images out. What effects do these images have
on the mood of the play here?

3 An unusual image (in pairs)

Hermia's image of the earth having a hole bored in it large enough for
the moon to pass through and then annoy the sun (the moon's
'brother') with 'th'Antipodes' (those who live on the opposite side of
the earth), is unusual to say the least. It is something like some of
Titania's speech in 2.1.81–117 in that it suggests everything in the
natural world is in disorder. Try writing your own image that
expresses the impossible (though, of course, Lysander *did* steal away
from Hermia). Do you think the language used by lovers is often full
of exaggeration?

I led them on in this distracted fear,
And left sweet Pyramus translated there;
When in that moment, so it came to pass,
Titania waked, and straightway loved an ass.
OBERON This falls out better than I could devise.   35
But hast thou yet latched the Athenian's eyes
With the love juice, as I did bid thee do?
PUCK I took him sleeping – that is finished too –
And the Athenian woman by his side,
That when he waked, of force she must be eyed.   40

Enter DEMETRIUS *and* HERMIA

OBERON Stand close: this is the same Athenian.
PUCK This is the woman, but not this the man.
DEMETRIUS O, why rebuke you him that loves you so?
Lay breath so bitter on your bitter foe.
HERMIA Now I but chide; but I should use thee worse,   45
For thou, I fear, hast given me cause to curse.
If thou hast slain Lysander in his sleep,
Being o'er shoes in blood, plunge in the deep,
And kill me too.
The sun was not so true unto the day   50
As he to me. Would he have stol'n away
From sleeping Hermia? I'll believe as soon
This whole earth may be bored, and that the moon
May through the centre creep, and so displease
Her brother's noontide with th'Antipodes.   55
It cannot be but thou hast murdered him:
So should a murderer look; so dead, so grim.
DEMETRIUS So should the murdered look, and so should I,
Pierced through the heart with your stern cruelty;
Yet you, the murderer, look as bright, as clear,   60
As yonder Venus in her glimmering sphere.
HERMIA What's this to my Lysander? Where is he?
Ah, good Demetrius, wilt thou give him me?
DEMETRIUS I had rather give his carcass to my hounds.

Hermia storms off, after accusing Demetrius of murder. Demetrius goes to sleep. Oberon tells Puck to find Helena in order to correct his mistake.

---

1 The lovers again (in groups of four to six)

Perhaps you have already discussed what the lovers were like in Act 1 (on page 16). Look again at Hermia and Demetrius here. Compare the two characters by listening to just his speeches, and then just her speeches. Discuss the differences between the two, perhaps comparing your impressions of them here with those earlier in the play.

2 The lovers again (2) (in groups of four to six)

Look again at the passage and page 71. It isn't just the lovers and the fairies that have different views of the world, but also Hermia and Demetrius. Make notes on what Hermia thinks is going on here, and what Demetrius thinks. Then relate it to how they are behaving.

3 Oberon (in pairs)

Read the final exchange between Puck and Oberon (lines 94–101). What does this tell you about Oberon and his motives in dealing with the mortals?

4 Are men fickle? (in pairs)

Puck says 'one man holding troth a million fail'. Debate whether men are fickle in love, and whether they are more fickle than women. Finally, look at the play itself, and whether the men are faithful in it.

---

misprision mistake
fancy-sick sick with love

HERMIA Out, dog! Out, cur! Thou driv'st me past the bounds   65
        Of maiden's patience. Hast thou slain him then?
        Henceforth be never numbered among men.
        O, once tell true; tell true, even for my sake:
        Durst thou have looked upon him being awake?
        And hast thou killed him sleeping? O, brave touch!   70
        Could not a worm, an adder do so much?
        An adder did it; for with doubler tongue
        Than thine, thou serpent, never adder stung.
DEMETRIUS You spend your passion on a misprised mood.
        I am not guilty of Lysander's blood,   75
        Nor is he dead, for aught that I can tell.
HERMIA I pray thee, tell me then that he is well.
DEMETRIUS And if I could, what should I get therefor?
HERMIA A privilege, never to see me more;
        And from thy hated presence part I so.   80
        See me no more, whether he be dead or no.   *Exit*
DEMETRIUS There is no following her in this fierce vein;
        Here therefore for a while I will remain.
        So sorrow's heaviness doth heavier grow
        For debt that bankrupt sleep doth sorrow owe,   85
        Which now in some slight measure it will pay,
        If for his tender here I make some stay.
            [He] lies down [and sleeps].
OBERON What hast thou done? Thou hast mistaken quite,
        And laid the love juice on some true love's sight.
        Of thy misprision must perforce ensue   90
        Some true love turned, and not a false turned true.
PUCK Then fate o'errules, that, one man holding troth,
        A million fail, confounding oath on oath.
OBERON About the wood go swifter than the wind,
        And Helena of Athens look thou find.   95
        All fancy-sick she is and pale of cheer
        With sighs of love, that costs the fresh blood dear.
        By some illusion see thou bring her here;
        I'll charm his eyes against she do appear.
PUCK I go, I go, look how I go!   100
        Swifter than arrow from the Tartar's bow.   *Exit*

Oberon puts the magic juice on Demetrius' eyes, and Lysander enters still trying to convince Helena he loves her. She thinks he's lying.

1 Puck
(in groups of four to six)

List the ways in which Puck behaves and thinks like a child, on the evidence here and elsewhere. He seems gleeful at the mayhem, and rather insensitive to the motives and feelings of the lovers. Compare all this with the illustration.

Puck (from an eighteenth-century book).

2 Audiences (in groups of four to six)

Find a space and act out this passage and the one on page 77. As actors, how do you want the audience to react to this? Empathy with Oberon and Puck gleefully watching the show, embarrassed and uncomfortable at seeing such strong emotions, or something else? Perhaps the presence of the fairies watching affects how we view things and the way we feel about the lovers.

3 The dance of the lovers – who loves whom?

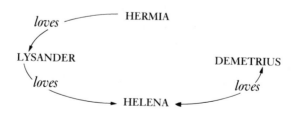

OBERON   [*Squeezing the juice on Demetrius' eyes.*]
       Flower of this purple dye,
       Hit with Cupid's archery,
       Sink in apple of his eye.
       When his love he doth espy,   105
       Let her shine as gloriously
       As the Venus of the sky.
       When thou wak'st, if she be by,
       Beg of her for remedy.

Enter PUCK

PUCK   Captain of our fairy band,   110
       Helena is here at hand,
       And the youth mistook by me,
       Pleading for a lover's fee.
       Shall we their fond pageant see?
       Lord, what fools these mortals be!   115
OBERON   Stand aside. The noise they make
       Will cause Demetrius to awake.
PUCK   Then will two at once woo one –
       That must needs be sport alone;
       And those things do best please me   120
       That befall prepost'rously.

Enter LYSANDER *and* HELENA

LYSANDER Why should you think that I should woo in scorn?
       Scorn and derision never come in tears.
     Look when I vow, I weep; and vows so born,
       In their nativity all truth appears.   125
     How can these things in me seem scorn to you,
     Bearing the badge of faith to prove them true?
HELENA You do advance your cunning more and more.
       When truth kills truth, O devilish-holy fray!
     These vows are Hermia's. Will you give her o'er?   130
       Weigh oath with oath, and you will nothing weigh;
     Your vows to her and me, put in two scales,
     Will even weigh, and both as light as tales.
LYSANDER I had no judgement when to her I swore.

Demetrius wakes and tells Helena how much he loves her, and she thinks he is part of the plot to tease her.

Helena, Lysander and Demetrius (Renaissance Theatre Company, 1990).

Taurus mountains in Turkey

HELENA Nor none, in my mind, now you give her o'er.   135
LYSANDER Demetrius loves her, and he loves not you.
DEMETRIUS (*Waking.*)
        O Helen, goddess, nymph, perfect, divine!
        To what, my love, shall I compare thine eyne?
        Crystal is muddy! O, how ripe in show
        Thy lips, those kissing cherries, tempting grow!   140
        That pure congealèd white, high Taurus' snow,
        Fanned with the eastern wind, turns to a crow
        When thou hold'st up thy hand. O, let me kiss
        This princess of pure white, this seal of bliss!
HELENA O spite! O Hell! I see you all are bent   145
        To set against me for your merriment.
        If you were civil, and knew courtesy,
        You would not do me thus much injury.
        Can you not hate me, as I know you do,
        But you must join in souls to mock me too?   150
        If you were men, as men you are in show,
        You would not use a gentle lady so,
        To vow, and swear, and superpraise my parts,
        When I am sure you hate me with your hearts.
        You both are rivals, and love Hermia;   155
        And now both rivals to mock Helena.
        A trim exploit, a manly enterprise,
        To conjure tears up in a poor maid's eyes
        With your derision! None of noble sort
        Would so offend a virgin, and extort   160
        A poor soul's patience, all to make you sport.

Lysander and Demetrius argue over Helena, and Hermia enters.
Hermia asks Lysander why he left her, and he says he hates her.

1 The lovers at war (in groups of four)

'Lovers' hardly seems an apt description here. There seem to be two arguments: one between Lysander and Demetrius, the other between Hermia and Lysander. Read through the passage a couple of times, developing the argument as you see fit, and then adding in the movement and gestures. Who, if anyone, has your sympathy, or who do you laugh at?

2 Magic and being 'amazed' (in groups of four to five)

If you were directing the passage opposite you might choose to discriminate between the 'magic'd' men and the 'amazed' women with their heads in reality. In your group, try out ideas of how to do this with one person as a director.

3 The last relationship fails (in groups of two to three)

Read through Helena's long speech on page 81 (lines 192–219). Look at the images of positive relationships and childhood, perhaps reading just those parts aloud. These seem a little out of place. Think carefully about why they might be here.

4 Onlookers (in groups of two to three)

Look at the photograph on page 80. Unless you are careful, it is easy to forget the presence of Oberon and Puck. This kind of voyeurism – sitting in on the pain and confusion of others – surely does not reflect well on them. Would it be possible to present these characters in a positive light here? How? Act out your ideas, concentrating solely on the involvement and response of Oberon and Puck.

---

sojourned travelled, stayed
aby pay
oes bright dress ornaments

LYSANDER You are unkind, Demetrius: be not so,
          For you love Hermia – this you know I know –
          And here with all good will, with all my heart,
          In Hermia's love I yield you up my part;   165
          And yours of Helena to me bequeath,
          Whom I do love, and will do till my death.
HELENA Never did mockers waste more idle breath.
DEMETRIUS Lysander, keep thy Hermia; I will none.
          If e'er I loved her, all that love is gone.   170
          My heart to her but as guest-wise sojourned,
          And now to Helen is it home returned,
          There to remain.
LYSANDER   Helen, it is not so.
DEMETRIUS Disparage not the faith thou dost not know,
          Lest to thy peril thou aby it dear.   175
          Look where thy love comes: yonder is thy dear.

                        Enter HERMIA

HERMIA Dark night, that from the eye his function takes,
          The ear more quick of apprehension makes;
          Wherein it doth impair the seeing sense
          It pays the hearing double recompense.   180
          Thou art not by mine eye, Lysander, found;
          Mine ear, I thank it, brought me to thy sound.
          But why unkindly didst thou leave me so?
LYSANDER Why should he stay whom love doth press to go?
HERMIA What love could press Lysander from my side?   185
LYSANDER Lysander's love, that would not let him bide,
          Fair Helena – who more engilds the night
          Than all yon fiery oes and eyes of light.
          [*To Hermia*] Why seek'st thou me? Could not this make
              thee know
          The hate I bare thee made me leave thee so?   190
HERMIA You speak not as you think; it cannot be.

Helena now thinks everyone is mocking her, and complains that Hermia should behave better as they have been such close friends for so long.

The lovers, Oberon and Puck (Renaissance Theatre Company, 1990).

sampler piece of embroidery

HELENA   Lo, she is one of this confederacy!
        Now I perceive they have conjoined all three
        To fashion this false sport in spite of me.
        Injurious Hermia, most ungrateful maid,   195
        Have you conspired, have you with these contrived
        To bait me with this foul derision?
        Is all the counsel that we two have shared,
        The sisters' vows, the hours that we have spent
        When we have chid the hasty-footed time   200
        For parting us – O, is all forgot?
        All schooldays' friendship, childhood innocence?
        We, Hermia, like two artificial gods
        Have with our needles created both one flower,
        Both on one sampler, sitting on one cushion,   205
        Both warbling of one song, both in one key,
        As if our hands, our sides, voices, and minds
        Had been incorporate. So we grew together
        Like to a double cherry, seeming parted,
        But yet an union in partition,   210
        Two lovely berries moulded on one stem;
        So with two seeming bodies but one heart,
        Two of the first, like coats in heraldry,
        Due but to one, and crownèd with one crest.
        And will you rent our ancient love asunder,   215
        To join with men in scorning your poor friend?
        It is not friendly, 'tis not maidenly.
        Our sex, as well as I, may chide you for it,
        Though I alone do feel the injury.
HERMIA   I am amazèd at your passionate words.   220
        I scorn you not; it seems that you scorn me.

Helena asks Hermia to have pity on her, and goes to leave because she's sure they are mocking her. Lysander offers to fight Demetrius for Helena.

1 Interviews (in groups of four to six)

Each take a part of one of the lovers. Write and rehearse a short monologue saying who you are, what has happened, how you feel, and what you want to happen. Don't forget the constraints of the flower's magic, the strange night-time woodland world the characters find themselves in, and their confused and emotional state. Video these monologues (if you can, otherwise just show them to the group). If you video them, try looking straight at the camera in a close-up.

This idea can be developed by having interviews of each of the lovers where feelings and thoughts are explored. This too could be on video, with the camera staying with the person interviewed.

2 Acting? Things are not as they seem
(in groups of two to three)

Look carefully at the part of Helena's speech that accuses the others of acting parts to deceive her (lines 237–9). Why did Shakespeare choose to use such an image here, and how does it relate to the rest of the play?

3 Men fighting over women (in groups of four to six)

This all seems rather stereotyped (and linked to the idea of male violence and male domination – why don't they just ask Helena?). But it seems to indicate that things are getting out of control. Predict some of the ways in which this conflict could end.

HELENA Have you not set Lysander, as in scorn,
         To follow me, and praise my eyes and face?
         And made your other love, Demetrius,
         Who even but now did spurn me with his foot,   225
         To call me goddess, nymph, divine and rare,
         Precious, celestial? Wherefore speaks he this
         To her he hates? And wherefore doth Lysander
         Deny your love, so rich within his soul,
         And tender me, forsooth, affection,   230
         But by your setting on, by your consent?
         What though I be not so in grace as you,
         So hung upon with love, so fortunate,
         But miserable most, to love unloved:
         This you should pity rather than despise.   235
HERMIA I understand not what you mean by this.
HELENA Ay, do! Persever, counterfeit sad looks,
         Make mouths upon me when I turn my back,
         Wink each at other, hold the sweet jest up.
         This sport, well carried, shall be chronicled.   240
         If you have any pity, grace, or manners,
         You would not make me such an argument.
         But fare ye well. 'Tis partly my own fault,
         Which death or absence soon shall remedy.
LYSANDER Stay, gentle Helena: hear my excuse,   245
         My love, my life, my soul, fair Helena!
HELENA O, excellent!
HERMIA [To Lysander] Sweet, do not scorn her so.
DEMETRIUS If she cannot entreat, I can compel.
LYSANDER Thou canst compel no more than she entreat;
         Thy threats have no more strength than her weak prayers.   250
         Helen, I love thee, by my life, I do:
         I swear by that which I will lose for thee
         To prove him false that says I love thee not.
DEMETRIUS I say I love thee more than he can do.
LYSANDER If thou say so, withdraw, and prove it too.   255
DEMETRIUS Quick, come.

Hermia clings on to Lysander as he insults her and tells her he hates her.

---

1 Lysander's insults (in pairs)

Make a list of Lysander's insulting descriptions of Hermia in lines 257–63 (leaving out the racist 'Ethiop' and 'tawny Tartar' – Elizabethans thought that a tan was unladylike, since ladies didn't walk much in the open air). One person then reads the list at the other: get as much venom in them as you can.

2 Hermia and Helena's insults (in pairs)

Try the same exercise as above, but with Hermia and Helena's insults (on page 87). It seems as if Hermia fears Helena insulting her because she is short. Discuss the attitudes current today about being tall and being short, and whether they are similar to the attitudes expressed here.

3 Love conceals, anger reveals (in groups of four to six)

Read through the argument between Hermia and Helena on page 87, and then consider whether or not their characters are revealed more clearly here than in Act 1 (where some might say only their love was apparent). Is it more complicated than this?

4 Violence (in pairs)

On page 87 there is a threat of the women fighting. Do your reactions to this differ from your reactions to the possibility of the men fighting – and why? Is it there purely for humour, or are there sinister undertones as well?

HERMIA   Lysander, whereto tends all this?
LYSANDER Away, you Ethiop!
DEMETRIUS   No, no, sir,
          Seem to break loose, take on as you would follow,
          But yet come not. You are a tame man, go.
LYSANDER Hang off, thou cat, thou burr! Vile thing, let loose,   260
          Or I will shake thee from me like a serpent.
HERMIA Why are you grown so rude? What change is this,
          Sweet love?
LYSANDER   Thy love? – out, tawny Tartar, out;
          Out, loathed medicine! O hated potion, hence!
HERMIA Do you not jest?
HELENA   Yes, sooth, and so do you.   265
LYSANDER Demetrius, I will keep my word with thee.
DEMETRIUS I would I had your bond, for I perceive
          A weak bond holds you. I'll not trust your word.
LYSANDER What? Should I hurt her, strike her, kill her dead?
          Although I hate her, I'll not harm her so.   270
HERMIA What? Can you do me greater harm than hate?
          Hate me? Wherefore? O me, what news, my love?
          Am not I Hermia? Are not you Lysander?
          I am as fair now as I was erewhile.
          Since night you loved me; yet since night you left me.   275
          Why then, you left me – O, the gods forbid! –
          In earnest, shall I say?
LYSANDER   Ay, by my life;
          And never did desire to see thee more.
          Therefore be out of hope, of question, of doubt;
          Be certain, nothing truer – 'tis no jest   280
          That I do hate thee and love Helena.

Hermia turns on Helena, and threatens to fight her, thinking Helena has stolen Lysander's love. Helena offers to return to Athens.

The lovers (New Shakespeare Company, 1980).

canker-blossom diseased flower

HERMIA [*To Helena*]
      O me, you juggler, you canker-blossom,
      You thief of love! What, have you come by night
      And stol'n my love's heart from him?
HELENA   Fine, i'faith!
      Have you no modesty, no maiden shame, 285
      No touch of bashfulness? What, will you tear
      Impatient answers from my gentle tongue?
      Fie, fie, you counterfeit, you puppet, you!
HERMIA 'Puppet'? Why so? – Ay, that way goes the game.
      Now I perceive that she hath made compare 290
      Between our statures; she hath urged her height,
      And with her personage, her tall personage,
      Her height, forsooth, she hath prevailed with him.
      And are you grown so high in his esteem
      Because I am so dwarfish and so low? 295
      How low am I, thou painted maypole? Speak!
      How low am I? I am not yet so low
      But that my nails can reach unto thine eyes.
HELENA I pray you, though you mock me, gentlemen,
      Let her not hurt me. I was never curst; 300
      I have no gift at all in shrewishness.
      I am a right maid for my cowardice;
      Let her not strike me. You perhaps may think
      Because she is something lower than myself
      That I can match her.
HERMIA   Lower? Hark, again! 305
HELENA Good Hermia, do not be so bitter with me.
      I evermore did love you, Hermia,
      Did ever keep your counsels, never wronged you,
      Save that in love unto Demetrius
      I told him of your stealth unto this wood. 310
      He followed you; for love I followed him,
      But he hath chid me hence, and threatened me
      To strike me, spurn me, nay, to kill me too.
      And now, so you will let me quiet go,
      To Athens will I bear my folly back, 315
      And follow you no further. Let me go;
      You see how simple and how fond I am.

*Helena explains her fear of 'little' Hermia. Lysander and Demetrius
leave to fight, Helena runs away, and Hermia follows.*

---

1 Scuffle? (in groups of four)

Obviously the men are keeping the women apart at one point at least
(line 328). Find your group a space and, getting your clues from the
speeches, work out what each character is doing – who is standing
where, to whom each speech is addressed, how to have the lovers
going off-stage, and so on. It's all very physical, and there are plenty
of good insults. Then act out this scene. A lot of actresses and actors
enjoy this part of the play – why?

2 Midsummer nightmare (in groups of two to four)

There are many nightmarish things about this play – being turned
into an ass, or Hermia's nightmare of the snake, for example. Perhaps
describe or paint/draw a
memorable dream you have had.
In groups, relate your dreams
and nightmares, and see if you
can analyse each other's. Discuss
whether you believe dreams have
any significance.

The Cry by Edvard Munch, 1895.

---

knot-grass a weed which was
  thought to stunt growth
aby pay for

coil turmoil
fray fight

HERMIA Why, get you gone! Who is't that hinders you?
HELENA A foolish heart that I leave here behind.
HERMIA What, with Lysander?
HELENA   With Demetrius.   320
LYSANDER Be not afraid; she shall not harm thee, Helena.
DEMETRIUS No, sir. She shall not, though you take her part.
HELENA O, when she is angry she is keen and shrewd;
     She was a vixen when she went to school,
     And though she be but little, she is fierce.   325
HERMIA Little again? Nothing but low and little?
     Why will you suffer her to flout me thus?
     Let me come to her.
LYSANDER   Get you gone, you dwarf,
     You minimus of hindering knot-grass made,
     You bead, you acorn.
DEMETRIUS   You are too officious   330
     In her behalf that scorns your services.
     Let her alone: speak not of Helena,
     Take not her part; for if thou dost intend
     Never so little show of love to her,
     Thou shalt aby it.
LYSANDER   Now she holds me not –   335
     Now follow, if thou dur'st, to try whose right,
     Of thine or mine, is most in Helena.
DEMETRIUS Follow? Nay, I'll go with thee, cheek by jowl.
                     Exeunt Lysander and Demetrius
HERMIA You, mistress, all this coil is 'long of you.
     Nay, go not back.
HELENA   I will not trust you, I,   340
     Nor longer stay in your curst company.
     Your hands than mine are quicker for a fray;
     My legs are longer, though, to run away!   *[Exit]*
HERMIA I am amazed, and know not what to say.   *Exit*

*Puck explains his mistake. Oberon instructs him to lead Lysander
and Demetrius astray by imitating their voices until all can be put right.*

---

1 It's not what you do, it's the way that you do it (in pairs)

Lines 354–77 are another example in the play of a long speech that
describes both speech and action. Explore some of the ways in which
Oberon and Puck could play this scene, paying particular attention to
what they do, and how they interact . . .

2 Puck and Oberon (in groups of three to four)

Pages 91 and 93 say a great deal about these two. Discuss whether
you believe Puck (lines 347–51), Puck's love of 'sport' and Oberon's
hope for 'all things shall be peace', and other points. Perhaps
Oberon's speech on page 93 (lines 388–95) says something about
both of them. Consider the photograph on page 92 too – perhaps
Oberon is manipulative but not malicious, or perhaps he has
Christ-like qualities of bringing love and harmony.

3 A promised restoration of order (in groups of three to four)

Look carefully at the language and imagery of pages 91 and 93.
Compare the writing here and the writing earlier in the scene, and the
power of some of the images to change how we are invited to look at
events ('seem a dream and fruitless vision'). Then think about the
audience and how they might react to the suggestion that everything
that has happened might seem like just a dream.

---

welkin sky
Acheron one of the rivers in
 Hades, the underworld for the
 dead

Oberon and Puck come forward.

OBERON This is thy negligence. Still thou mistak'st,   345
   Or else committ'st thy knaveries wilfully.
PUCK Believe me, King of Shadows, I mistook.
   Did not you tell me I should know the man
   By the Athenian garments he had on?
   And so far blameless proves my enterprise   350
   That I have 'nointed an Athenian's eyes;
   And so far am I glad it so did sort,
   As this their jangling I esteem a sport.
OBERON Thou seest these lovers seek a place to fight:
   Hie therefore, Robin, overcast the night;   355
   The starry welkin cover thou anon
   With drooping fog as black as Acheron,
   And lead these testy rivals so astray
   As one come not within another's way.
   Like to Lysander sometime frame thy tongue,   360
   Then stir Demetrius up with bitter wrong,
   And sometime rail thou like Demetrius;
   And from each other look thou lead them thus,
   Till o'er their brows death-counterfeiting sleep
   With leaden legs and batty wings doth creep.   365
   Then crush this herb into Lysander's eye,
   Whose liquor hath this virtuous property,
   To take from thence all error with his might,
   And make his eyeballs roll with wonted sight.
   When they next wake, all this derision   370
   Shall seem a dream and fruitless vision,
   And back to Athens shall the lovers wend
   With league whose date till death shall never end.
   Whiles I in this affair do thee employ
   I'll to my Queen and beg her Indian boy;   375
   And then I will her charmèd eye release
   From monster's view, and all things shall be peace.

Day approaches, and though the fairies (unlike other spirits) can exist in the day, Oberon urges haste. Lysander returns and is misled by Puck.

Oberon and Puck (New Shakespeare Company, 1989).

Aurora's harbinger signal of the dawn – the morning star

Neptune god of the sea. The morning sun's beams turn the sea from green to 'yellow gold', transforming it

PUCK My fairy lord, this must be done with haste,
For night's swift dragons cut the clouds full fast,
And yonder shines Aurora's harbinger,   380
At whose approach ghosts wandering here and there
Troop home to churchyards. Damnèd spirits all,
That in crossways and floods have burial,
Already to their wormy beds are gone.
For fear lest day should look their shames upon,   385
They wilfully themselves exile from light,
And must for aye consort with black-browed night.
OBERON But we are spirits of another sort.
I with the morning's love have oft made sport,
And like a forester the groves may tread   390
Even till the eastern gate, all fiery-red,
Opening on Neptune with fair blessèd beams,
Turns into yellow gold his salt green streams.
But notwithstanding, haste, make no delay;
We may effect this business yet ere day.   [*Exit*]   395
PUCK   Up and down, up and down,
I will lead them up and down;
I am feared in field and town.
Goblin, lead them up and down.
Here comes one.   400

Enter LYSANDER

LYSANDER Where art thou, proud Demetrius? Speak thou now.
PUCK Here, villain, drawn and ready! Where art thou?
LYSANDER I will be with thee straight.
PUCK   Follow me then
To plainer ground.

[Exit Lysander]

93

Puck misleads both Demetrius and Lysander by imitating their voices until they both fall asleep.

---

1 Sleep sound (in groups of five)

Start by considering how Puck should imitate Lysander's voice well enough to fool Demetrius (and, a little later, imitate Demetrius' own voice). Then read through pages 95 and 97, working out how to get all the lovers asleep near one another. Try your ideas out. This can be extended by videoing the same scene. The camera close-ups will let you do the voices in quite a different way, presenting different problems and offering a variety of opportunities to experiment. You might then compare the two versions.

2 To sleep, perchance to dream

Although there has been a night and dreams, at the end of pages 95 and 97 the lovers are asleep. Write down the thoughts and feelings of each as they drift into sleep, or write about his/her dreams.

3 Men versus women (in pairs)

Compare the speeches on pages 95 and 97 of the male lovers with those of the female lovers. One read the male speeches, one the female. You may think it relevant and interesting to look at what Puck says here as well. Join with another group and share your findings.

4 The world of the woods (in groups of five)

Create a display that shows how you think the world of the woods should look (using drawings, photographs, images from Acts 2 and 3 and so on). Do the same for the lovers (and see pages 8, 76 and 86).

---

recreant coward, villain
wot know

Enter DEMETRIUS

DEMETRIUS   Lysander, speak again.
        Thou runaway, thou coward, art thou fled?   405
        Speak! In some bush? Where dost thou hide thy head?
PUCK Thou coward, art thou bragging to the stars,
        Telling the bushes that thou look'st for wars,
        And wilt not come? Come, recreant, come, thou child,
        I'll whip thee with a rod. He is defiled   410
        That draws a sword on thee.
DEMETRIUS   Yea, art thou there?
PUCK Follow my voice. We'll try no manhood here.

                                                          Exeunt

        Enter LYSANDER

LYSANDER He goes before me, and still dares me on;
        When I come where he calls, then he is gone.
        The villain is much lighter-heeled than I;   415
        I followed fast, but faster he did fly,
        That fallen am I in dark uneven way,
        And here will rest me. (*Lies down.*) Come, thou gentle day,
        For if but once thou show me thy grey light
        I'll find Demetrius and revenge this spite. [*Sleeps.*]   420

        Enter PUCK *and* DEMETRIUS

PUCK Ho, ho, ho! Coward, why com'st thou not?
DEMETRIUS Abide me if thou dar'st, for well I wot
        Thou runn'st before me, shifting every place,
        And dar'st not stand nor look me in the face.
        Where art thou now?
PUCK   Come hither; I am here.   425
DEMETRIUS Nay then, thou mock'st me. Thou shalt buy this dear
        If ever I thy face by daylight see.
        Now, go thy way; faintness constraineth me
        To measure out my length on this cold bed.
        By day's approach look to be visited. [*Sleeps.*]   430

*Helena and Hermia enter separately, exhausted, and fall asleep.
Puck puts the magic juice on Lysander's eyes to make him love
Hermia again.*

1 A look at metre (in groups of two to three)

Look at the speeches on pages 95 and 97. Compare the way in which
the speeches here are written with the couplets on page 93. You can
see that the speeches of Helena and Hermia are in the same rhyming
pattern, but that Puck uses quite a different pattern of verse (**metre**).
Pick one pattern of verse each from this page, and write your own
poem (on any topic you wish) that fits the pattern as exactly as you can
make it. Then read Shakespeare's aloud, and read yours. Talk about
what you discover both in the writing and in the reading of the poems.

2 Puck – a knavish lad (in groups of two to three)

Look closely at what Puck says about women in lines 435–41 and
453–63. What kind of attitude does he appear to have towards them?

3 The lovers come together in peace?
(in groups of two or three)

Somehow, after the conflicts of Acts 1, 2 and 3, the lovers are now
united (if only physically here, we know it will be emotionally when
they awake). On a literal level, this is because of the fairies. What
might it be on other levels? You can look at the ideas at the end of this
book, page 152 if you like.

4 The awakening (in groups of four)

Improvise a scene immediately following this where the lovers wake
up, and discover that they are now neatly sorted out into couples.

Enter HELENA

HELENA O weary night, O long and tedious night,
    Abate thy hours, shine comforts from the east,
    That I may back to Athens by daylight
    From these that my poor company detest;
    And sleep, that sometimes shuts up sorrow's eye,   435
    Steal me awhile from mine own company. (*Sleeps.*)
PUCK   Yet but three? Come one more,
    Two of both kinds makes up four.
    Here she comes, curst and sad.
    Cupid is a knavish lad   440
    Thus to make poor females mad.

Enter HERMIA

HERMIA Never so weary, never so in woe,
    Bedabbled with the dew, and torn with briars –
    I can no further crawl, no further go;
    My legs can keep no pace with my desires.   445
    Here will I rest me till the break of day.
    Heavens shield Lysander, if they mean a fray. [*Sleeps.*]
PUCK   On the ground
    Sleep sound.
    I'll apply   450
    To your eye,
    Gentle lover, remedy.
    [*Squeezes the juice on Lysander's eyes.*]
    When thou wak'st,
    Thou tak'st
    True delight   455
    In the sight
    Of thy former lady's eye;
    And the country proverb known,
    That every man should take his own,
    In your waking shall be shown.   460
    Jack shall have Jill,
    Naught shall go ill:
    The man shall have his mare again, and all shall be well.
    [*Exit Puck;*] *the lovers remain on stage, asleep*

A Midsummer Night's Dream

Bottom and Titania (Royal Shakespeare Company, 1962).

Bottom gives instructions to Titania's fairies.

Bottom, Titania and the fairies (Renaissance Theatre Company, 1990).

coy caress
neaf fist
cavalery a gentleman (Bottom's
  mistake for 'cavalier')

tongs . . . bones simple musical
  instruments

ACT 4   SCENE 1
The wood

Enter TITANIA, Queen of Fairies, and BOTTOM, and fairies
[including PEASEBLOSSOM, COBWEB and MUSTARDSEED;] and the
King OBERON behind them

TITANIA Come, sit thee down upon this flowery bed
　　　　While I thy amiable cheeks do coy,
　　　　And stick musk-roses in thy sleek smooth head,
　　　　And kiss thy fair large ears, my gentle joy.

BOTTOM Where's Peaseblossom?　　　　　　　　　　　　　　　5

PEASEBLOSSOM Ready.

BOTTOM Scratch my head, Peaseblossom. Where's Mounsieur
　　　Cobweb?

COBWEB Ready.

BOTTOM Mounsieur Cobweb, good Mounsieur, get you your weapons　10
　　　in your hand, and kill me a red-hipped humble-bee on the top of
　　　a thistle; and, good Mounsieur, bring me the honey-bag. Do not
　　　fret yourself too much in the action, Mounsieur; and, good
　　　Mounsieur, have a care the honey-bag break not; I would be loath
　　　to have you overflown with a honey-bag, signior. Where's Moun-　15
　　　sieur Mustardseed?

MUSTARDSEED Ready.

BOTTOM Give me your neaf, Mounsieur Mustardseed. Pray you, leave
　　　your courtesy, good Mounsieur.

MUSTARDSEED What's your will?　　　　　　　　　　　　　20

BOTTOM Nothing, good Mounsieur, but to help Cavalery Peaseblossom
　　　to scratch. I must to the barber's, Mounsieur, for methinks I am
　　　marvellous hairy about the face. And I am such a tender ass, if my
　　　hair do but tickle me, I must scratch.

TITANIA What, wilt thou hear some music, my sweet love?　　　　25

BOTTOM I have a reasonable good ear in music. Let's have the tongs
　　　and the bones.

TITANIA Or say, sweet love, what thou desir'st to eat.

BOTTOM Truly, a peck of provender, I could munch your good dry oats.
　　　Methinks I have a great desire to a bottle of hay. Good hay, sweet　30
　　　hay hath no fellow.

Bottom and Titania sleep. Oberon talks to Puck about his pity for Titania and how she has returned the changeling boy. He removes the spell on her and wakes her.

1 Bottom (in groups of four)

Read through the speeches on page 101. Bottom has changed in the way he looks, but he also seems to have changed in other ways. Find as many examples of these changes as you can, and talk about how they might be put across on stage, then . . .

2 Fairies (in groups of four)

'The minute you say "fairy" to people, they think they know exactly what it is.' Siobhan Redmond (Titania in the Renaissance Theatre Company Production, 1990)

Discuss the possibilities:

- fairies at the bottom of the garden
- non-human spirits
- a way of bringing on stage the world of fantasy and imagination
- representatives of magical and spiritual forces in human lives.

To help you decide what you think, look at the illustrations on pages 24, 25, 32, 98, 99 and 100, consider the fairies' names, and look at what they do in the play. Present your conclusions to the class.

3 'The fierce vexation of a dream' (in groups of four)

Discuss this description of the night's events from the lovers' point of view, and from the point of view of the other characters. Take each of the main words in lines 64–6 into account.

4 Seeing or imagining? (in groups of four)

One person reads Oberon's speech while the rest mime to it. Then act out Oberon speaking to Puck only. Which do you feel is more effective: seeing or imagining?

---

exposition of another of Bottom's mistakes; surely he means disposition to?

woodbine bindweed
swain lover

TITANIA I have a venturous fairy that shall seek
　　　　The squirrel's hoard, and fetch thee new nuts.
BOTTOM I had rather have a handful or two of dried peas. But, I pray
　　　　you, let none of your people stir me; I have an exposition of sleep   35
　　　　come upon me.
TITANIA Sleep thou, and I will wind thee in my arms.
　　　　Fairies be gone, and be all ways away.   [*Exeunt Fairies*]
　　　　So doth the woodbine the sweet honeysuckle
　　　　Gently entwist; the female ivy so   40
　　　　Enrings the barky fingers of the elm.
　　　　O, how I love thee! How I dote on thee!
　　　　　　　[*They sleep.*]

　　　　　Enter PUCK. OBERON *comes forward*

OBERON Welcome, good Robin. Seest thou this sweet sight?
　　　　Her dotage now I do begin to pity;
　　　　For, meeting her of late behind the wood   45
　　　　Seeking sweet favours for this hateful fool,
　　　　I did upbraid her and fall out with her,
　　　　For she his hairy temples then had rounded
　　　　With coronet of fresh and fragrant flowers;
　　　　And that same dew, which sometime on the buds   50
　　　　Was wont to swell like round and orient pearls,
　　　　Stood now within the pretty flowerets' eyes
　　　　Like tears that did their own disgrace bewail.
　　　　When I had at my pleasure taunted her,
　　　　And she in mild terms begged my patience,   55
　　　　I then did ask of her her changeling child,
　　　　Which straight she gave me, and her fairy sent
　　　　To bear him to my bower in Fairyland.
　　　　And now I have the boy, I will undo
　　　　This hateful imperfection of her eyes.   60
　　　　And, gentle Puck, take this transformèd scalp
　　　　From off the head of this Athenian swain,
　　　　That, he awaking when the other do,
　　　　May all to Athens back again repair,
　　　　And think no more of this night's accidents   65
　　　　But as the fierce vexation of a dream.
　　　　But first I will release the Fairy Queen.
　　　　　　[*Squeezing a herb on Titania's eyes.*]

Titania and Oberon are reconciled. Puck removes the ass's head from Bottom. All leave except the 'mortals' (the lovers and Bottom).

---

1 'Methought I was enamoured of an ass' (in pairs)

One person act as Titania, waking from her vision, the other Oberon. Improvise Titania's thoughts and feelings in a speech that tells Oberon about her 'vision', and then Oberon's comments and replies.

2 Music and dance (in pairs)

The resolution of the conflict between Titania and Oberon is marked by both dance and music. In Elizabethan times the harmony of music was often taken as a symbol or sign of human harmony. What kind of music and dance would be suitable for this moment in the play? If you can, develop a short dance of Titania and Oberon, perhaps to some appropriate music you have found.

3 The fairies, lovers and Bottom (in groups of four to six)

At this moment, all of these characters are in the same place ('all these five' are the lovers and Bottom on the ground). Discuss whether having all the characters together is significant, and why.

4 The language of Oberon (in pairs)

Look carefully at Oberon's speech (lines 82–9), and the language that he uses. How is it different from the language of his first speeches in Act 2 (see page 31)? Think of the possible reasons for this.

5 'Trip we after night's shade' (in groups of four to six)

The transition between the page opposite and page 107 is between the fairy world of moonlight and the daylight world of Theseus. How might you signal this change on stage? (Lighting and scenery might provide a useful starting point.)

   Be as thou wast wont to be;
   See as thou wast wont to see.
   Dian's bud o'er Cupid's flower   70
   Hath such force and blessèd power.
  Now, my Titania, wake you, my sweet Queen!

TITANIA *[Starting up.]*
   My Oberon, what visions have I seen!
   Methought I was enamoured of an ass.

OBERON There lies your love.

TITANIA   How came these things to pass? 75
   O, how mine eyes do loathe his visage now!

OBERON Silence awhile: Robin, take off this head.
   Titania, music call, and strike more dead
   Than common sleep of all these five the sense.

TITANIA Music, ho, music such as charmeth sleep! 80
      [Soft music plays.]

PUCK *[To Bottom, removing the ass's head]*
   Now when thou wak'st, with thine own fool's eyes peep.

OBERON Sound, music! Come, my Queen, take hands with me,
   And rock the ground whereon these sleepers be.
      [They dance.]
   Now thou and I are new in amity,
   And will tomorrow midnight solemnly 85
   Dance in Duke Theseus' house triumphantly,
   And bless it to all fair prosperity.
   There shall the pairs of faithful lovers be
   Wedded, with Theseus, all in jollity.

PUCK   Fairy King, attend, and mark: 90
   I do hear the morning lark.

OBERON   Then, my Queen, in silence sad,
   Trip we after night's shade;
   We the globe can compass soon,
   Swifter than the wandering moon. 95

TITANIA Come, my lord, and in our flight
   Tell me how it came this night
   That I sleeping here was found
   With these mortals on the ground.
     Exeunt Oberon, Titania and Puck

Theseus, Hippolyta, Egeus and others enter on an early morning hunting expedition. They find the sleeping lovers.

1 A sound picture? (in groups of three to four)

A number of speeches present a scene or picture in words. What kind of picture is presented in lines 100–23, and what aspects of the audience's imagination are called on to make it real?

2 'The rite of May' (in groups of three to four)

There is a connection here with the festivals of Tudor England (as there is in the title of the play itself). In some of these festivals, ordinary behaviour and laws were dispensed with. Festivals could include disorder and people behaving in very unusual ways, free of ordinary constraints. In a way, it is like the modern holiday where people go to escape everyday life and do things they wouldn't ordinarily do. Talk about how people can behave on holiday (including yourself), and then compare that with how people behave in the play.

3 A word of warning

Is the sudden remembrance of the threat (lines 132–4) to put Hermia in a convent or execute her a real worry here?

4 Can't Shakespeare count? (in pairs)

The play opens with 'Four days will quickly steep themselves in night four nights will quickly dream away the time', but now Hermia has to give her answer the next morning. Seems a bit harsh: can't Shakespeare count? Suggest reasons why Shakespeare might have done this. Also, how do they observe the 'rite of May' on a midsummer's night? Or doesn't it matter?

---

vaward early part
Hercules the mythical Greek hero, famed for his strength

Cadmus mythical founder of Thebes
so flewed, so sanded with similar jowls and similar sandy colouring

Wind horns. Enter THESEUS *with* HIPPOLYTA, EGEUS, *and all his train.*

THESEUS Go, one of you, find out the forester;   100
       For now our observation is performed,
       And since we have the vaward of the day,
       My love shall hear the music of my hounds.
       Uncouple in the western valley; let them go:
       Dispatch, I say, and find the forester.   105
                                 [Exit an Attendant]
       We will, fair Queen, up to the mountain's top,
       And mark the musical confusion
       Of hounds and echo in conjunction.
HIPPOLYTA I was with Hercules and Cadmus once,
       When in a wood of Crete they bayed the bear   110
       With hounds of Sparta: never did I hear
       Such gallant chiding; for besides the groves,
       The skies, the fountains, every region near
       Seemed all one mutual cry. I never heard
       So musical a discord, such sweet thunder.   115
THESEUS My hounds are bred out of the Spartan kind,
       So flewed, so sanded; and their heads are hung
       With ears that sweep away the morning dew;
       Crook-kneed, and dewlapped like Thessalian bulls;
       Slow in pursuit, but matched in mouth like bells,   120
       Each under each. A cry more tuneable
       Was never hallooed to nor cheered with horn
       In Crete, in Sparta, nor in Thessaly.
       Judge when you hear. But soft, what nymphs are these?
EGEUS My lord, this is my daughter here asleep,   125
       And this Lysander; this Demetrius is,
       This Helena, old Nedar's Helena.
       I wonder of their being here together.
THESEUS No doubt they rose up early to observe
       The rite of May, and hearing our intent   130
       Came here in grace of our solemnity.
       But speak, Egeus; is not this the day
       That Hermia should give answer of her choice?
EGEUS It is, my lord.

The lovers are awoken, and, as Lysander tries to explain what
has happened, Egeus urges the Duke to punish Lysander for eloping.

---

1 Three speeches, three views (in groups of three)

Each take a part, and read this page aloud, thinking about the mood of each character. Together, look at each of the character's speeches, especially the language and images each uses. Finally, present the state of mind of each character in a short monologue.

2 The dance of the lovers – who loves whom?
(in groups of three)

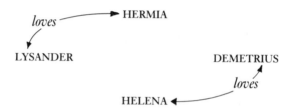

This is the final arrangement of the lovers. Look back through the play at the notes on the 'dance' of the lovers (pages 10, 50 and 74). Putting all the dances together, look at what pattern emerges. You might then apply this to the play, looking for patterns of day/night; Athens/wood; and others. Make charts/graphs/displays of your findings, and include any explanations that you have. (See page 153.)

3 What do you think of Egeus? (in groups of three)

A simple enough question – answer it.

4 Back to the beginning? (in groups of three)

Has the play now come full circle, with Egeus demanding his 'rights' and nothing changing, the whole 'dream' having had no effect on the real world, or . . .?

---

couple pair up

THESEUS Go, bid the huntsmen wake them with their horns.   135
     Shout within; wind horns; [the lovers] all start up.
     Good morrow, friends. Saint Valentine is past;
     Begin these woodbirds but to couple now?
     [The lovers kneel.]
LYSANDER Pardon, my lord.
THESEUS   I pray you all, stand up.
     I know you two are rival enemies:
     How comes this gentle concord in the world,   140
     That hatred is so far from jealousy
     To sleep by hate, and fear no enmity?
LYSANDER My lord, I shall reply amazedly,
     Half sleep, half waking; but as yet, I swear,
     I cannot truly say how I came here.   145
     But as I think (for truly would I speak)
     And now I do bethink me, so it is –
     I came with Hermia hither. Our intent
     Was to be gone from Athens, where we might
     Without the peril of the Athenian law –   150
EGEUS Enough, enough, my lord; you have enough –
     I beg the law, the law upon his head!
     They would have stol'n away, they would, Demetrius,
     Thereby to have defeated you and me,
     You of your wife, and me of my consent,   155
     Of my consent that she should be your wife.

Demetrius explains his new-found love for Helena. Theseus instructs the lovers to come with him to be married. All leave except the lovers.

---

1 Demetrius – another view? (in pairs)

Compare Demetrius' speech here with one of his earlier speeches. Pick one speech each, and read one then the other, trying to bring out Demetrius' mood and character. Go through each speech, picking out the words and phrases that best capture his personality (e.g. 'I in fury'), and read just those parts of the speeches. How has he changed – and why?

2 'Love' and 'dote' (in small groups)

Demetrius says his feeling for Hermia was mere 'doting', and his feeling for Helena is now 'love'. Draw up a list of which relationships in different parts of the play you think were 'doting' and which 'love'. Then prepare a short presentation for the class involving the whole group that gives your view of the difference between the two feelings using this speech and others where you can.

3 Theseus and Oberon (in groups of four to six)

Here Theseus is the dominant character (but also look at 1.1.83–90 and other parts in the play). Read some of these speeches aloud and then compare them with some of Oberon's. Go on to talk about and list the similarities and differences between the two characters. Do you feel the fairy and mortal worlds are dominated by men, or is it more complicated than that?

---

idle gaud worthless toy

DEMETRIUS My lord, fair Helen told me of their stealth,
　　　　　Of this their purpose hither to this wood;
　　　　　And I in fury hither followed them,
　　　　　Fair Helena in fancy following me.　　　　　　　160
　　　　　But, my good lord, I wot not by what power
　　　　　(But by some power it is), my love to Hermia,
　　　　　Melted as the snow, seems to me now
　　　　　As the remembrance of an idle gaud
　　　　　Which in my childhood I did dote upon;　　　　165
　　　　　And all the faith, the virtue of my heart,
　　　　　The object and the pleasure of mine eye,
　　　　　Is only Helena. To her, my lord,
　　　　　Was I betrothed ere I saw Hermia;
　　　　　But like a sickness did I loathe this food.　　　170
　　　　　But, as in health come to my natural taste,
　　　　　Now I do wish it, love it, long for it,
　　　　　And will for evermore be true to it.
THESEUS Fair lovers, you are fortunately met.
　　　　　Of this discourse we more will hear anon.　　　175
　　　　　Egeus, I will overbear your will;
　　　　　For in the temple, by and by, with us
　　　　　These couples shall eternally be knit.
　　　　　And, for the morning now is something worn,
　　　　　Our purposed hunting shall be set aside.　　　180
　　　　　Away with us to Athens. Three and three,
　　　　　We'll hold a feast in great solemnity.
　　　　　Come, Hippolyta.
　　　　　　　　Exit Theseus with Hippolyta, Egeus, and his train

The lovers wonder if they are dreaming, agree they are awake, and follow the Duke. Bottom awakes and wonders at his 'dream'.

---

1 Reading through (in groups of five)

Each take a part and read through the passage. Then find yourself a space and 'walk through' the passage as you read. Examine different ways of acting it out, especially the appropriate movement from all the actors, especially when they are *not* speaking.

2 It's not what you say, it's the way that you say it (in pairs)

Read the lovers' speeches (lines 184–96), and then Bottom's (lines 197–211), and talk about the differences in the way they describe their experiences. You might like to compare Bottom's speech with *1 Corinthians 2 v.9* in the Bible:

> But as it is written, Eye hath not seen, nor ear heard, neither have entered into the heart of man, the things which God hath prepared for them that love him.

There are also parallels with Titania's dazed state (in Act 4, Scene 1, lines 73–99). The different worlds of the fairies, lovers and the Mechanicals all meet at this point – or do they?

3 Newsflash (in small groups)

Video or act out a television news report with an interview and/or newspaper report with the four lovers (or Bottom), on romance and marriage, and their strange experiences in the woods. Create two reports: one in the style of a popular newspaper that prints scandal and the other in the style of a serious newspaper.

4 Bottom's dream (in large groups)

Write and perform your own version of this, as described in lines 206–11.

DEMETRIUS These things seem small and undistinguishable,
　　Like far-off mountains turnèd into clouds.　　　　　　　185
HERMIA Methinks I see these things with parted eye,
　　When everything seems double.
HELENA　　　　　　　　　　　　So methinks;
　　And I have found Demetrius, like a jewel,
　　Mine own, and not mine own.
DEMETRIUS　　　　　　　　　　Are you sure
　　That we are awake? It seems to me　　　　　　　　　190
　　That yet we sleep, we dream. Do not you think
　　The Duke was here, and bid us follow him?
HERMIA Yea, and my father.
HELENA　　　　　　　And Hippolyta.
LYSANDER And he did bid us follow to the temple.
DEMETRIUS Why, then, we are awake. Let's follow him,　　　195
　　And by the way let us recount our dreams.

　　　　　　　　　　　　　　　　　　Exeunt lovers

　　　　　　　　Bottom wakes.

BOTTOM When my cue comes, call me, and I will answer. My next is
'Most fair Pyramus'. Heigh ho! Peter Quince? Flute the bellows-
mender? Snout the tinker? Starveling? God's my life! Stolen hence
and left me asleep! I have had a most rare vision. I have had a dream,　　200
past the wit of man to say what dream it was. Man is but an ass
if he go about to expound this dream. Methought I was – there is
no man can tell what. Methought I was – and methought I had – but
man is but a patched fool if he will offer to say what methought
I had. The eye of man hath not heard, the ear of man hath not seen,　　205
man's hand is not able to taste, his tongue to conceive, nor his heart
to report what my dream was! I will get Peter Quince to write a
ballad of this dream; it shall be called 'Bottom's Dream', because
it hath no bottom; and I will sing it in the latter end of a play, before
the Duke. Peradventure, to make it the more gracious, I shall sing　　210
it at her death.　　　　　　　　　　　　　　　　　　*Exit*

The Mechanicals, without Bottom, despair (they had been looking forward to a regular salary from the Duke for their work); but Bottom suddenly arrives with the news that their play has been chosen.

The Mechanicals (Hull Truck Theatre Company, 1987).

paramour . . . thing of naught a mistress and, to Flute, something immoral and wicked

made men our fortunes would be made

ACT 4 SCENE 2
Athens

Enter QUINCE, FLUTE, SNOUT and STARVELING

QUINCE Have you sent to Bottom's house? Is he come home yet?

STARVELING He cannot be heard of. Out of doubt he is transported.

FLUTE If he come not, then the play is marred. It goes not forward.
Doth it?

QUINCE It is not possible. You have not a man in all Athens able to   5
discharge Pyramus but he.

FLUTE No, he hath simply the best wit of any handicraft man in Athens.

QUINCE Yea, and the best person, too; and he is a very paramour for
a sweet voice.

FLUTE You must say 'paragon'. A paramour is (God bless us!) a thing   10
of naught.   *Enter* SNUG *the joiner*

SNUG Masters, the Duke is coming from the temple, and there is two
or three lords and ladies more married. If our sport had gone
forward, we had all been made men.

FLUTE O, sweet bully Bottom! Thus hath he lost sixpence a day during   15
his life: he could not have 'scaped sixpence a day. And the Duke
had not given him sixpence a day for playing Pyramus, I'll be
hanged. He would have deserved it. Sixpence a day in Pyramus,
or nothing.   *Enter* BOTTOM

BOTTOM Where are these lads? Where are these hearts?   20

QUINCE Bottom! O most courageous day! O most happy hour!

BOTTOM Masters, I am to discourse wonders – but ask me not what;
for if I tell you, I am not true Athenian. I will tell you everything,
right as it fell out.

QUINCE Let us hear, sweet Bottom.   25

BOTTOM Not a word of me. All that I will tell you is – that the Duke
hath dined. Get your apparel together, good strings to your beards,
new ribbons to your pumps: meet presently at the palace, every man
look o'er his part. For the short and the long is, our play is preferred.
In any case, let Thisbe have clean linen; and let not him that plays   30
the lion pare his nails, for they shall hang out for the lion's claws.
And, most dear actors, eat no onions nor garlic; for we are to utter
sweet breath, and I do not doubt but to hear them say it is a sweet
comedy. No more words. Away! Go, away!   *Exeunt*

A Midsummer Night's Dream

Snug and Snout (BBC, 1971).

The Mechanicals' play (Renaissance Theatre Company, 1990).

*Theseus and Hippolyta talk about the lovers' story, and the power
of imagination in poet, lover and madman, who all see things that
are not there.*

1 Theseus versus Hippolyta (in pairs)

Taking a part each, read the speeches on the page opposite. Then
compare their two judgements of the 'story of the night' and what it
says about each character. You may already have compared the lovers'
and Bottom's reactions to the night (page 112). Making some kind of
display or presentation to the others, bring out how each character
reacts – and thinks about – the midsummer night's dream.

2 Do you believe in fairies? (full class debate)

Even in Shakespeare's day, belief in fairies wasn't the norm for
educated people. Debate the statement, 'Ghosts, poltergeists and all
things supernatural exist only in the imagination'.

3 Do you believe in fairies? (2) (in groups of four)

Many people think the fairies in this play represent what might be
called a 'magical' or 'spiritual' side of our life, or even the power of
imagination. Discuss how three types of people might react to seeing
A Midsummer Night's Dream and its fairies – a Mechanical-type
person (a worker), a lover (a teenager in love), and a ruler like
Theseus (a politician). Then improvise a scene of these three people
leaving the theatre being interviewed about the play and what they
thought of it.

4 *A Midsummer Night's Dream* itself
(in groups of two or three)

Theseus speaks of the imagination of a number of kinds of people,
including 'the poet', like Shakespeare himself. Look at Theseus'
description of what the poet does (lines 12–17), and discuss whether
you think it describes *A Midsummer Night's Dream* itself. You might
then go on to examine what part the imaginations of 'lovers' and
'lunatics' have in the play.

---

toys tales
compact composed

ACT 5 SCENE 1
Athens Theseus' Palace

Enter THESEUS, HIPPOLYTA, PHILOSTRATE, *Lords and Attendants*

HIPPOLYTA 'Tis strange, my Theseus, that these lovers speak of.
THESEUS More strange than true. I never may believe
These antique fables, nor these fairy toys.
Lovers and madmen have such seething brains,
Such shaping fantasies, that apprehend   5
More than cool reason ever comprehends.
The lunatic, the lover, and the poet
Are of imagination all compact:
One sees more devils than vast hell can hold;
That is the madman. The lover, all as frantic,   10
Sees Helen's beauty in a brow of Egypt.
The poet's eye, in a fine frenzy rolling,
Doth glance from heaven to earth, from earth to heaven;
And as imagination bodies forth
The forms of things unknown, the poet's pen   15
Turns them to shapes, and gives to airy nothing
A local habitation and a name.
Such tricks hath strong imagination
That if it would but apprehend some joy,
It comprehends some bringer of that joy;   20
Or in the night, imagining some fear,
How easy is a bush supposed a bear?
HIPPOLYTA But all the story of the night told over,
And all their minds transfigured so together,
More witnesseth than fancy's images,   25
And grows to something of great constancy;
But howsoever, strange and admirable.

The lovers enter, and Theseus looks through the list of plays ready for the evening's entertainment.

The stage audience (New Shakespeare Company, 1983).

masques dances or entertainments
  where masks were worn
abridgement pastime; to make
  time go quickly
brief a summary

Enter the lovers: LYSANDER, DEMETRIUS, HERMIA *and* HELENA

THESEUS Here come the lovers, full of joy and mirth.
　　　　Joy, gentle friends, joy and fresh days of love
　　　　Accompany your hearts!
LYSANDER　　　　　　　More than to us   30
　　　　Wait in your royal walks, your board, your bed!
THESEUS Come now: what masques, what dances shall we have
　　　　To wear away this long age of three hours
　　　　Between our after-supper and bedtime?
　　　　Where is our usual manager of mirth?   35
　　　　What revels are in hand? Is there no play
　　　　To ease the anguish of a torturing hour?
　　　　Call Philostrate.
PHILOSTRATE　　　　　Here, mighty Theseus.
THESEUS Say, what abridgement have you for this evening?
　　　　What masque, what music? How shall we beguile   40
　　　　The lazy time if not with some delight?
PHILOSTRATE [*Giving him a paper.*]
　　　　There is a brief how many sports are ripe.
　　　　Make choice of which your highness will see first.
THESEUS [*Reading.*]
　　　　'The battle with the Centaurs, to be sung
　　　　By an Athenian eunuch to the harp' –   45
　　　　We'll none of that; that have I told my love
　　　　In glory of my kinsman, Hercules.
　　　　[*Reading.*] 'The riot of the tipsy Bacchanals,
　　　　Tearing the Thracian singer in their rage' –
　　　　That is an old device, and it was played   50
　　　　When I from Thebes came last a conqueror.
　　　　[*Reading.*] 'The thrice three Muses mourning for the death
　　　　Of learning, late deceased in beggary' –
　　　　That is some satire keen and critical,
　　　　Not sorting with a nuptial ceremony.   55
　　　　[*Reading.*] 'A tedious brief scene of young Pyramus
　　　　And his love Thisbe, very tragical mirth' –
　　　　Merry and tragical? Tedious and brief?
　　　　That is hot ice and wondrous strange snow!
　　　　How shall we find the concord of this discord?   60

Theseus decides on the Mechanicals' play despite the objections of Philostrate, who says the rehearsal was laughably bad.

1 Is Philostrate being fair? (in groups of four)

Examine Philostrate's description of the Mechanicals and their play, and consider whether you think he is being fair to them.

2 Audience one, audience two (in groups of four)

The Mechanicals will perform to two audiences: the Court, and the audience watching *A Midsummer Night's Dream*. We get an outsider's view of the Mechanicals' play here – look at Philostrate's description (lines 61–70), and try to think of reasons why Shakespeare included this description of the play when both audiences were about to see it anyway. Would both audiences react in the same way to the Mechanicals' play? Report back to the class on your conclusions.

3 Seeing the play on 29 September 1662

Samuel Pepys saw the play on this date and wrote:

> 'and then to the King's Theatre, where we saw *Midsummer Night's Dreame*, which I have never seen before, nor shall ever again, for it is the most insipid ridiculous play that I ever saw in my life.'

Do you think this fits the Mechanicals' play better than the whole play? Write down your reasons.

---

unbreathed unpractised
conned learnt

wretchedness o'ercharged those of little ability overstretched

PHILOSTRATE A play there is, my lord, some ten words long,
    Which is as 'brief' as I have known a play,
    But by ten words, my lord, it is too long,
    Which makes it 'tedious'. For in all the play
    There is not one word apt, one player fitted.   65
    And 'tragical', my noble lord, it is,
    For Pyramus therein doth kill himself,
    Which when I saw rehearsed, I must confess,
    Made mine eyes water; but more 'merry' tears
    The passion of loud laughter never shed.   70
THESEUS What are they that do play it?
PHILOSTRATE Hard-handed men that work in Athens here,
    Which never laboured in their minds till now;
    And now have toiled their unbreathed memories
    With this same play against your nuptial.   75
THESEUS And we will hear it.
PHILOSTRATE   No, my noble lord,
    It is not for you. I have heard it over,
    And it is nothing, nothing in the world,
    Unless you can find sport in their intents,
    Extremely stretched, and conned with cruel pain,   80
    To do you service.
THESEUS   I will hear that play;
    For never anything can be amiss
    When simpleness and duty tender it.
    Go bring them in; and take your places, ladies.
            [*Exit Philostrate*]
HIPPOLYTA I love not to see wretchedness o'ercharged,   85
    And duty in his service perishing.
THESEUS Why, gentle sweet, you shall see no such thing.
HIPPOLYTA He says they can do nothing in this kind.

Theseus explains his choice: it is the thought that counts among simple people. Quince then enters and begins the play, rather strangely.

---

1 The Mechanicals' play (in small groups)

Look at the photographs from productions (pages 116, 117 and 140) and decide how you would present the Mechanicals' play. (See page 150.)

2 On show (in small groups)

We are all on show to others every time we are in public. But great occasions can stop us speaking altogether. In lines 93–105 Theseus talks about learned people such as 'great clerks' being unable to talk during official welcomes. He also criticises 'audacious eloquence', those who speak perhaps a little too well in public. He seems to prefer 'love' (in the wider sense of deep affection) and 'tongue-tied simplicity', those who speak a little ('least') but communicate a great deal ('speak most'). Describe occasions when you as individuals have had to speak in public or have been intimidated by a group or person.

3 Well said! (in pairs)

Quince's Prologue (lines 108–17) has much of its punctuation in the wrong place (that's why the Court joke about his 'points' and 'stops' – the punctuation). One person practise the speech as it is written (bearing in mind what the audience says), and the other try to re-punctuate the speech to make better sense. Then read the two versions one after another – which works best?

4 Asides (in groups of four)

Discuss whether Quince hears the comments of the Court (lines 118–23), or whether they are asides (heard only by the audience). Try acting it out both ways: if Quince hears, he will react; if he doesn't, he will have to be doing something – even if only standing still. Keep this in mind for the rest of the Mechanicals' play.

---

in might, not merit accepts it given the ability of those that offer it
periods stops
capacity understanding
addressed ready

stand upon points take notice of punctuation or detail
stop a pun on full stop, and suddenly stopping a horse when riding
in government under control

THESEUS The kinder we, to give them thanks for nothing.
        Our sport shall be to take what they mistake;   90
        And what poor duty cannot do, noble respect
        Takes it in might, not merit.
        Where I have come, great clerks have purposèd
        To greet me with premeditated welcomes,
        Where I have seen them shiver and look pale,   95
        Make periods in the midst of sentences,
        Throttle their practised accent in their fears,
        And in conclusion dumbly have broke off,
        Not paying me a welcome. Trust me, sweet,
        Out of this silence yet I picked a welcome,   100
        And in the modesty of fearful duty
        I read as much as from the rattling tongue
        Of saucy and audacious eloquence.
        Love, therefore, and tongue-tied simplicity
        In least speak most, to my capacity.   105

Enter PHILOSTRATE

PHILOSTRATE So please your grace, the Prologue is addressed.
THESEUS Let him approach.
        Flourish of trumpets.

Enter QUINCE *as Prologue*

QUINCE   If we offend, it is with our good will.
        That you should think, we come not to offend,
        But with good will. To show our simple skill,   110
        That is the true beginning of our end.
        ⁀Consider then, we come but in despite.
        We do not come as minding to content you,
        Our true intent is. All for your delight,
        We are not here. That you should here repent you,   115
        The actors are at hand; and by their show
        You shall know all that you are like to know.
THESEUS This fellow doth not stand upon points.
LYSANDER He hath rid his prologue like a rough colt; he knows not
    the stop. A good moral, my lord; it is not enough to speak, but to   120
    speak true.
HIPPOLYTA Indeed, he hath played on this prologue like a child on
    a recorder – a sound, but not in government.

Quince gives the Prologue, which explains the play, and introduces the characters.

---

1 Mime to the Prologue (in groups of six or more)

Read aloud Quince's Prologue (lines 126–50) a few times, thinking about what the other Mechanicals and the stage audience might be doing. Identify points in the speech which seem to indicate something happening on stage ('at this show' or 'this man is Pyramus'). What other actions might be appropriate?

Mime along with the Prologue (which can be read by the person playing Quince), developing each character's actions and reactions. Try different ways of doing this: completely over-the-top, stumbling and muddled, or in any other way which you think might work. Choose your favourite version and present it to the class.

2 The play itself (in small groups)

From the Prologue, discuss what kind of play it is, how it is described by Quince, and what this tells us about the Mechanicals and their ideas about what a play should be.

3 A quick thought

Compare this speech (lines 126–50) to Quince's last one (lines 108–117). Think about how they are different – and why.

THESEUS His speech was like a tangled chain, nothing impaired, but
all disordered. Who is next?   125

Enter with a Trumpeter before them [BOTTOM *as*] *Pyramus,* [FLUTE *as*]
Thisbe, [SNOUT *as*] *Wall,* [STARVELING *as*] *Moonshine and* [SNUG *as*]
Lion.

QUINCE (*as Prologue*)
    Gentles, perchance you wonder at this show,
        But wonder on, till truth make all things plain.
    This man is Pyramus, if you would know;
        This beauteous lady Thisbe is, certain.
    This man with lime and rough-cast doth present   130
        Wall, that vile wall which did these lovers sunder;
    And through Wall's chink, poor souls, they are content
        To whisper – at the which let no man wonder.
    This man with lanthorn, dog, and bush of thorn,
        Presenteth Moonshine; for, if you will know,   135
    By moonshine did these lovers think no scorn
        To meet at Ninus' tomb, there, there to woo.
    This grisly beast, which Lion hight by name,
    The trusty Thisbe, coming first by night,
    Did scare away, or rather did affright;   140
    And as she fled, her mantle she did fall,
        Which Lion vile with bloody mouth did stain.
    Anon comes Pyramus, sweet youth and tall,
        And finds his trusty Thisbe's mantle slain;
    Whereat with blade, with bloody, blameful blade,   145
        He bravely broached his boiling bloody breast;
    And Thisbe, tarrying in mulberry shade,
        His dagger drew, and died. For all the rest,
    Let Lion, Moonshine, Wall, and lovers twain
    At large discourse, while here they do remain.   150
           Exeunt Quince, Bottom, Flute, Snug and Starveling

Snout, as the Wall, explains his role. Bottom, as Pyramus, enters and begins the play's action.

---

1 Bottom's up (in pairs)

Everyone needs to have a chance to be Bottom – take turns acting out his speech (lines 167–78) – your partner can be the admiring Wall.

2 O speech, O speech so full of O's (in pairs)

Have a close look at Bottom's speech and all the repetitions of words and ideas. Think of some way of showing these repetitions (written or spoken).

3 O speech beyond compare (in pairs)

Compare Bottom's speech (lines 167–78) to Snout's (lines 153–62). Write down the differences, and what they suggest about each character.

4 Did you say something? (in pairs)

What do you make of the last two speeches (lines 179–82)? Try different ways of acting them out (perhaps starting with the last four lines of Bottom's speech as Pyramus).

5 A quick thought

Look at the comments made about the players and the play, and note down what sort of attitude the Court has to the Mechanicals' play.

---

curse again should curse back,
  since it is 'sensible' (alive)

THESEUS I wonder if the lion be to speak?

DEMETRIUS No wonder, my lord; one lion may, when many asses do.

SNOUT (*as Wall*)

    In this same interlude it doth befall

    That I, one Snout by name, present a wall;

    And such a wall as I would have you think   155

    That had in it a crannied hole or chink,

    Through which the lovers, Pyramus and Thisbe,

    Did whisper often, very secretly.

    This loam, this rough-cast, and this stone doth show

    That I am that same wall; the truth is so.   160

    And this the cranny is, right and sinister,

    Through which the fearful lovers are to whisper.

THESEUS Would you desire lime and hair to speak better?

DEMETRIUS It is the wittiest partition that ever I heard discourse, my
lord.   165

Enter BOTTOM *as* PYRAMUS

THESEUS Pyramus draws near the wall; silence!

BOTTOM (*as Pyramus*)

    O grim-looked night, O night with hue so black,

       O night which ever art when day is not!

    O night, O night, alack, alack, alack,

       I fear my Thisbe's promise is forgot!   170

    And thou, O wall, O sweet, O lovely wall,

       That stand'st between her father's ground and mine,

    Thou wall, O wall, O sweet and lovely wall,

       Show me thy chink, to blink through with mine eyne.

        [*Wall parts his fingers.*]

    Thanks, courteous wall; Jove shield thee well for this!   175

       But what see I? No Thisbe do I see.

    O wicked wall, through whom I see no bliss,

       Cursed be thy stones for thus deceiving me!

THESEUS The wall, methinks, being sensible, should curse again.

BOTTOM No, in truth sir, he should not. 'Deceiving me' is Thisbe's   180
cue. She is to enter now, and I am to spy her through the wall.
You shall see it will fall pat as I told you. Yonder she comes.

Thisbe and Pyramus declare their love for each other through the wall, and agree to meet at 'Ninny's tomb'.

---

1 Gooseberry (in groups of three)

Start by looking at Flute and 'her' speeches opposite, thinking about 'her' voice and actions. Talk about Bottom's speeches, then the gooseberry, or odd one out: Snout as Wall, and how he is reacting to the other two. Finally, get up and act this scene out, trying out different ways of doing the scene.

2 Watch your language (in pairs)

Write down a list of words used in Thisbe's first speech (lines 183–6) that are not really used today (with a separate list for any that are used in a way they aren't used today). Replace them in the speech with modern words or phrases that mean the same thing. Remember that some things change because Shakespeare's world was different from ours ('stones with lime and hair knit up in thee' isn't the same as pre-mixed concrete and bricks!). So change those images to modern images. Read both versions of the speech aloud (the original and your modern version) and compare them.

3 Lovers (in small groups)

In this passage, Pyramus and Thisbe compare themselves to many different famous lovers (though they get the names wrong). Compare them with the lovers in *A Midsummer Night's Dream*. Discuss whether young love should be treated seriously or whether there can be a funny side to it – for outsiders.

Limander, Helen this should be Leander and Hero, two legendary lovers

Shafalus, Procrus this should be Cephalus and Procris, other legendary lovers
tide come

Enter FLUTE *as* THISBE

FLUTE (*as Thisbe*)
>O wall, full often hast thou heard my moans,
>>For parting my fair Pyramus and me.
>My cherry lips have often kissed thy stones,   185
>>Thy stones with lime and hair knit up in thee.

BOTTOM (*as Pyramus*)
>I see a voice; now will I to the chink,
>>To spy and I can hear my Thisbe's face.
>Thisbe!

FLUTE (*as Thisbe*)
>>My love! Thou art my love, I think?

BOTTOM (*as Pyramus*)
>Think what thou wilt, I am thy lover's grace,   190
>And like Limander am I trusty still.

FLUTE (*as Thisbe*)
>And I like Helen, till the Fates me kill.

BOTTOM (*as Pyramus*)
>Not Shafalus to Procrus was so true.

FLUTE (*as Thisbe*)
>As Shafalus to Procrus, I to you.

BOTTOM (*as Pyramus*)
>O, kiss me through the hole of this vile wall!   195

FLUTE (*as Thisbe*)
>I kiss the wall's hole, not your lips at all.

BOTTOM (*as Pyramus*)
>Wilt thou at Ninny's tomb meet me straightway?

FLUTE (*as Thisbe*)
>Tide life, tide death, I come without delay.
>>>>*[Exeunt Bottom and Flute in different directions]*

*The stage audience comment on the play, and Snug (the lion)
enters, explaining that he is not really a lion.*

---

1 The audience (in groups of four to six)

Read out the page opposite, paying careful attention to the stage
audience's remarks. Try different ways of playing these parts,
concentrating on the tone of the speakers, and how the tone brings
out their attitude to the play and judgement of it.

2 Give each line its due (in small groups)

Hippolyta says 'This is the silliest stuff that ever I heard' – do you as a
group agree with this? Compare this with what Pepys said (page 122).
Theseus, in his reply, talks about all plays ('The best in this kind are
but shadows') – what might he mean? Talk about what Theseus says
in lines 208–10 and whether you agree with him. Share your
conclusions on all these points with the class.

3 Give each part its due (in pairs)

Take it in turns to act out Snug's part (lines 211–18 in particular).
Karl James, who played Snug in the Renaissance Theatre Company's
production (see page 117) rushed round the watching Court handing
out his business cards when he came to the phrase 'I as Snug the
joiner am'. Invent other stage 'business' that might develop this
speech and this character.

---

mural wall
fox . . . goose the lion was
  supposed to be brave, the fox
  cunning (discretion), and the goose
  stupid

SNOUT (*as Wall*)
> Thus have I, Wall, my part dischargèd so;
> And being done, thus Wall away doth go.   *Exit*   200

THESEUS Now is the mural down between the two neighbours.

DEMETRIUS No remedy, my lord, when walls are so wilful to hear without warning.

HIPPOLYTA This is the silliest stuff that ever I heard.

THESEUS The best in this kind are but shadows; and the worst are no   205
worse, if imagination amend them.

HIPPOLYTA It must be your imagination then, and not theirs.

THESEUS If we imagine no worse of them than they of themselves, they
may pass for excellent men. Here come two noble beasts in, a man
and a lion.   210

> *Enter [Snug as] Lion and [Starveling as] Moonshine.*

SNUG (*as Lion*)
> You ladies, you whose gentle hearts do fear
> > The smallest monstrous mouse that creeps on floor,
> May now, perchance, both quake and tremble here,
> > When Lion rough in wildest rage doth roar.
> Then know that I as Snug the joiner am   215
> A lion fell, nor else no lion's dam;
> For if I should as lion come in strife
> Into this place, 'twere pity on my life.

THESEUS A very gentle beast, and of a good conscience.

DEMETRIUS The very best at a beast, my lord, that e'er I saw.   220

LYSANDER This lion is a very fox for his valour.

THESEUS True; and a goose for his discretion.

DEMETRIUS Not so, my lord; for his valour cannot carry his discretion;
and the fox carries the goose.

THESEUS His discretion, I am sure, cannot carry his valour; for the   225
goose carries not the fox. It is well: leave it to his discretion, and
let us listen to the moon.

Starveling, as the Moon, explains his role, despite the comments of the stage audience. Thisbe arrives only to run away from the lion.

---

1 The unruly audience (in groups of six to eight)

The stage audience seems to be getting out of hand here. Taking parts, read through the passage a couple of times. Come to some conclusions about Starveling seeming to give up on speaking his lines, and on how the audience is behaving. Look too at the end of this section, where the audience even seems to be shouting out ironic comments like a football crowd. Try different ways to bring all this out when you act it out, and then show your version to the class.

2 Imagining the moon (in small groups)

The image of the moon is common throughout *A Midsummer Night's Dream*. Find some of the references to the moon and compare them with the presentation of the moon here. You might like to discuss the differences between what we as the audience are asked to do in the whole play (imagine both the moon and its effects from just Shakespeare's words), and what the Mechanicals think their audience needs. Perhaps the Mechanicals look down on the understanding and imagination of their audience, just as their audience looks down on them. Discuss some ideas of what the Court would have presented as a play for the Mechanicals (perhaps if they had used the story of Pyramus and Thisbe). Improvise a small part of such a play, and show it to the class.

---

horns on his head the sign of a cuckold (someone whose wife has been unfaithful)

well moused the lion is like a cat with a mouse (the mantle)

STARVELING (*as Moonshine*)
      This lanthorn doth the hornèd moon present –
DEMETRIUS He should have worn the horns on his head.
THESEUS He is no crescent, and his horns are invisible within the   230
      circumference.
STARVELING (*as Moonshine*)
      This lanthorn doth the hornèd moon present;
            Myself the man i'th'moon do seem to be –
THESEUS This is the greatest error of all the rest; the man should be
      put into the lantern. How is it else the man i'th'moon?   235
DEMETRIUS He dares not come there, for the candle; for you see it is
      already in snuff.
HIPPOLYTA I am aweary of this moon. Would he would change!
THESEUS It appears by his small light of discretion that he is in the
      wane; but yet in courtesy, in all reason, we must stay the time.   240
LYSANDER Proceed, Moon.
STARVELING All that I have to say is to tell you that the lanthorn is
      the moon, I the man i'th'moon, this thorn bush my thorn bush,
      and this dog my dog.
DEMETRIUS Why, all these should be in the lantern, for all these are   245
      in the moon. But silence: here comes Thisbe.

                  Enter [FLUTE *as*] THISBE

FLUTE (*as Thisbe*)
      This is old Ninny's tomb. Where is my love?
SNUG (*as Lion*) O!
                        Lion roars. Thisbe runs off [*dropping her mantle*]
DEMETRIUS Well roared, Lion!
THESEUS Well run, Thisbe!   250
HIPPOLYTA Well shone, Moon! Truly, the moon shines with a good
      grace.
THESEUS Well moused, Lion!
DEMETRIUS And then came Pyramus –
LYSANDER And so the lion vanished.   255
                  [*Lion worries Thisbe's mantle, and exit*]

Pyramus enters full of expectation. He then sees Thisbe's blood-stained mantle.

---

1 Bottom as an actor (in small groups)

Read the comments on Bottom's acting (lines 272–4). Compare Bottom as an actor and Bottom as a character and the relationship between the two.

2 'I pity the man'

Peter Brook's 1979 production had one actress playing both Titania and Hippolyta, and implied that there was a sexual relationship between Titania and Bottom (see page 66). When the actress came to line 274, she made it obvious that she was recalling the night's activities. Do you think it would work to have one actress playing these two parts?

3 Every trick in the book? (in pairs)

Start by reading Bottom's speech (lines 256–271) to each other. Look at the speech again as if you were Shakespeare, thinking about what you've put in the speech to make Bottom appear ridiculous. Make a list of such 'tricks' of language and rhyme, explaining if you can what sort of 'tricks' Shakespeare is using (the activities on page 128 might help you get started).

4 Shakespeare 2, the sequel (in groups of two to three)

Think about the story of Pyramus and Thisbe, and pick a moment the Mechanicals left out (say, when Pyramus and Thisbe's parents hear of their deaths). Work together to write the speeches using Shakespeare's tricks to make it ridiculous. Display them in the classroom, and act them out.

Fates, thread and thrum the goddesses controlling lives, spinning out the threads of people's lives, and ending them by cutting the thread (and thrum)

beshrew my heart exclamation, like 'Bless my soul!'

Enter BOTTOM *as* PYRAMUS

BOTTOM (*as Pyramus*)
        Sweet moon, I thank thee for thy sunny beams;
          I thank thee, moon, for shining now so bright;
        For by thy gracious, golden, glittering gleams
          I trust to take of truest Thisbe sight.
               But stay – O spite!   260
               But mark, poor Knight,
            What dreadful dole is here?
              Eyes, do you see?
              How can it be?
           O dainty duck, O dear!   265
              Thy mantle good –
           What, stained with blood?
          Approach, ye Furies fell!
             O Fates, come, come,
             Cut thread and thrum,   270
         Quail, crush, conclude, and quell.
THESEUS This passion, and the death of a dear friend, would go near
    to make a man look sad.
HIPPOLYTA Beshrew my heart, but I pity the man.

Pyramus stabs himself, and has a prolonged death. As the audience comments on the acting, Thisbe enters.

---

1 Who has the best part? (in pairs)

Compare Bottom's last speech (lines 275–90) with Thisbe's (on page 141), perhaps starting by looking for any ridiculous images and ideas, but going on to acting them out. There's a good deal to think about in what each actor is doing (especially for a line like 'Now die, die, die, die, die!').

2 A good-looking girl, that Thisbe

Take a good look at the man playing Flute (Thisbe) in the photograph on page 140 (it is Gerard Horan). Think about whether you like the image he puts across, and what Flute might be like if played by other very different-looking actors.

3 An ass by any other name . . . (in small groups)

Yet again, someone implies that Bottom is an 'ass' (line 294). With a name like Bottom, and having an ass's head at one point, this idea of his character is pretty clear. Look here and elsewhere in the play at what Bottom says and does, and make a list of reasons why Bottom is – or isn't – an ass.

4 'Your play needs no excuse' (in groups of four to six)

Discuss whether the Mechanicals' play needs excusing (line 335), and then look again at the plays Theseus had a choice of viewing (see 5.1. 44–60). Decide in your group whether Theseus' choice was wise, bearing in mind how the audience reacted to the Mechanicals' play. Report back to the rest of the class with your conclusions.

---

pap breast
die one of a pair of dice; an ace (one) is the lowest throw (Demetrius puns on Bottom's use of 'die')

mote minute particle
means, videlicet moans, makes a formal legal complaint

BOTTOM (*as Pyramus*)

    O wherefore, Nature, didst thou lions frame,   275
      Since lion vile hath here deflowered my dear?
    Which is – no, no – which was the fairest dame
        That lived, that loved, that liked, that looked with cheer.
           Come tears, confound!
           Out sword, and wound   280
        The pap of Pyramus,
          Ay, that left pap,
          Where heart doth hop:
    Thus die I, thus, thus, thus! [*Stabs himself.*]
         Now am I dead,   285
         Now am I fled;
       My soul is in the sky.
         Tongue, lose thy light;
         Moon, take thy flight;

                     [*Exit Starveling*]

    Now die, die, die, die, die. [*He dies.*]   290

DEMETRIUS No die, but an ace for him; for he is but one.

LYSANDER Less than an ace, man; for he is dead, he is nothing.

THESEUS With the help of a surgeon he might yet recover, and yet prove an ass.

HIPPOLYTA How chance Moonshine is gone before Thisbe comes back   295
and finds her lover?

THESEUS She will find him by starlight.

         Enter [FLUTE *as*] THISBE

Here she comes and her passion ends the play.

HIPPOLYTA Methinks she should not use a long one for such a
Pyramus; I hope she will be brief.   300

DEMETRIUS A mote will turn the balance, which Pyramus, which
Thisbe is the better: he for a man, God warrant us; she for a woman,
God bless us.

LYSANDER She hath spied him already, with those sweet eyes.

DEMETRIUS And thus she means, videlicet –   305

Thisbe realises Pyramus is dead and kills herself. Bottom asks if the Duke wants an epilogue or a dance, and the Duke asks for a dance.

The Mechanicals' play (Renaissance Theatre Company, 1990).

sisters three the Fates (see the
  gloss on page 136)
shore shorn

imbrue stab
Bergomask a country dance

FLUTE (*as Thisbe*)

    Asleep, my love?
    What, dead, my dove?
O Pyramus, arise.
    Speak, speak! Quite dumb?
    Dead, dead? A tomb   310
Must cover thy sweet eyes.
    These lily lips,
    This cherry nose,
These yellow cowslip cheeks
    Are gone, are gone.   315
    Lovers, make moan;
His eyes were green as leeks.
    O sisters three,
    Come, come to me
With hands as pale as milk;   320
    Lay them in gore,
    Since you have shore
With shears his thread of silk.
    Tongue, not a word!
    Come, trusty sword,   325
Come blade, my breast imbrue! [*Stabs herself.*]
    And farewell, friends.
    Thus Thisbe ends –
    Adieu, adieu, adieu! [*Dies.*]

THESEUS Moonshine and Lion are left to bury the dead.   330

DEMETRIUS Ay, and Wall, too.

BOTTOM [*Starting up, as Flute does also.*] No, I assure you, the wall is down that parted their fathers. Will it please you to see the epilogue, or to hear a Bergomask dance between two of our company?

THESEUS No epilogue, I pray you; for your play needs no excuse. Never   335
excuse; for when the players are all dead, there need none to be blamed. Marry, if he that writ it had played Pyramus and hanged himself in Thisbe's garter, it would have been a fine tragedy: and so it is, truly, and very notably discharged. But come, your Bergomask; let your epilogue alone.   340

The Mechanicals dance, the Duke instructs everyone to go to bed, and Puck enters.

---

1 The dance (in groups of five)

It was quite common for plays to end with a dance in Shakespeare's day. The Bergomask was a country dance, but using any kind of music you think suitable work out a dance for the Mechanicals.

2 Puck's world

Make an illustration of Puck's speech (lines 349–69), based on the images there. Again, Shakespeare lets us imagine this visual scene. Write about the difference between your illustration and Puck's words. You could put different illustrations up on display.

3 A different mood? (in pairs)

One person read Theseus' speech, the other Puck's. Think carefully about differences between them, particularly in mood and images, in the feel they give to the play. Read the two speeches again, this time with actions, trying to emphasise those differences between them. If you were directing the play, what would you do with the lighting during lines 348–9? Contrast Puck's world and the world of Theseus at this moment.

4 All together now: one, two, three . . . (in pairs)

Here the Mechanicals, the Court, and fairies are in the same place in quick succession. How would the three groups look back on the events of the play?

---

palpable-gross uncouth
foredone worn out

wasted brands burnt logs
triple Hecate's team the moon's chariot

[The company return; two of them dance, then exeunt Bottom, Flute and their fellows.]

The iron tongue of midnight hath told twelve.
Lovers, to bed; 'tis almost fairy time.
I fear we shall outsleep the coming morn
As much as we this night have overwatched.
This palpable-gross play hath well beguiled   345
The heavy gait of night. Sweet friends, to bed.
A fortnight hold we this solemnity
In nightly revels and new jollity.

Exeunt

Enter PUCK *[carrying a broom]*

PUCK   Now the hungry lion roars,
            And the wolf behowls the moon,   350
        Whilst the heavy ploughman snores,
            All with weary task foredone.
        Now the wasted brands do glow,
            Whilst the screech-owl, screeching loud,
        Puts the wretch that lies in woe   355
            In remembrance of a shroud.
        Now it is the time of night
            That the graves, all gaping wide,
        Every one lets forth his sprite
            In the church-way paths to glide.   360
        And we fairies, that do run
            By the triple Hecate's team
        From the presence of the sun,
            Following darkness like a dream,
        Now are frolic; not a mouse   365
        Shall disturb this hallowed house.
        I am sent with broom before
        To sweep the dust behind the door.

*Oberon and Titania, with their fairies, enter, and Oberon
instructs them to go through the house, blessing the three couples with
loving marriages and 'perfect' children.*

1 Watch your language (in groups of three)

The lovers are middle-class and the Mechanicals workers, and
Shakespeare makes their language very different. For the fairies,
Shakespeare uses the language of country myths, or even certain
kinds of literature. Write a modern blessing in the manner of
Oberon's (lines 379–400). Compare it with Oberon's speech and a
blessing from the *Book of Common Prayer* (1662) on marriage and
children:

> We beseech thee, assist with thy blessing these two persons, that
> they may both be fruitful in procreation of children, and also live
> together so long in godly love and honesty, that they may see their
> children christianly and virtuously brought up, to thy praise and
> honour; through Jesus Christ our Lord.

2 The dance again (in groups of six or more)

Picking your own music, improvise and develop a dance (and song) to
suit the fairies and the moment in the play. Perform it for the rest of
the class.

3 'Sweet peace' (in groups of four to six)

Compare the speeches here with the conflicts of the opening scene
and the conflicts in the wood, noting down the differences. Everyone
is brought together in the same place (Theseus' palace), and the
marriages are blessed. In the play there are many relationships
between women and men, all of which have had problems. What has
brought them to 'sweet peace' now? For each couple, find explanations of how their problems have been resolved. Look at the spiritual
or mental changes, as well as the way the plot works.

---

mark prodigious birthmark which
  is ominous
take his gait go his way

Enter [OBERON *and* TITANIA,] *the King and Queen of Fairies, with all*
their train.

OBERON   Through the house give glimmering light
                By the dead and drowsy fire;   370
            Every elf and fairy sprite
                Hop as light as bird from briar,
            And this ditty after me
            Sing, and dance it trippingly.

TITANIA   First rehearse your song by rote,   375
            To each word a warbling note;
            Hand in hand with fairy grace
            Will we sing and bless this place.
                        Song [*and dance*].

OBERON   Now until the break of day
            Through this house each fairy stray.   380
            To the best bride-bed will we,
            Which by us shall blessèd be;
            And the issue there create
            Ever shall be fortunate.
            So shall all the couples three   385
            Ever true in loving be,
            And the blots of nature's hand
            Shall not in their issue stand.
            Never mole, harelip, nor scar,
            Nor mark prodigious, such as are   390
            Despisèd in nativity,
            Shall upon their children be.
            With this field-dew consecrate,
            Every fairy take his gait,
            And each several chamber bless   395
            Through this palace with sweet peace;
            And the owner of it blessèd
            Ever shall in safety rest.
            Trip away, make no stay;
            Meet me all by break of day.   400
                        Exeunt [*all but Puck*]

Puck, on his own now, asks for the audience's approval.

---

1 Shakespeare's audience (in groups of four to six)

Shakespeare's audience would, apparently, either hiss ('the serpent's tongue') or clap ('give us your hands') at the end of plays. Plays often ended with a request to the audience to clap (and not hiss!). Is Puck the right person to ask the audience for their applause, and the right person to end the play?

2 Exploring patterns (in groups of two to three)

Look very closely at the words Puck uses in lines 401–08, and group his words into patterns ('shadows', 'slumbered', 'visions', 'dream' might be one). Relate these patterns to the play as a whole.

3 What are plays anyway? (in groups of four to six)

The Mechanicals have shown their play. *A Midsummer Night's Dream* ends with Shakespeare calling the actors 'shadows' (line 401) and the play itself 'visions'.

Discuss what plays (and films and drama on television) actually are, and why people still like to watch such 'visions' and 'dreams'.

4 Whose dream? (in groups of four to six)

The lovers and Bottom have already been involved in experiences that they think are dreams. Now Puck suggests we consider the whole play as 'but a dream' that we have experienced as an audience. Whose 'dream' is the play – ours, Shakespeare's, the mortals in the play, all of these, or . . .?

---

restore amends Puck will, in
return, make amends

PUCK [*To the audience*]

    If we shadows have offended,
    Think but this, and all is mended:
    That you have but slumbered here
    While these visions did appear;
    And this weak and idle theme,   405
    No more yielding but a dream,
    Gentles, do not reprehend;
    If you pardon, we will mend.
    And, as I am an honest Puck,
    If we have unearnèd luck   410
    Now to 'scape the serpent's tongue
    We will make amends ere long,
    Else the Puck a liar call.
    So, good night unto you all.
    Give me your hands, if we be friends,   415
    And Robin shall restore amends.   [*Exit*]

Puck (Hull Truck Theatre Company, 1987).

A Midsummer Night's Dream in production
Starting points for class, group and individual work

'You don't do a play to neaten it up, to whip it into shape: you do it to release it, to unleash it from the page. It's up to you what to make of it.'
Siobhan Redmond (Titania and Hippolyta in the Renaissance Theatre Company production)

An ideal way to explore the play is to take part in a production of it. This would mean making many key decisions: where the play is set (ancient Athens? modern Grimsby?), how the fairies are to be presented, how the play should be cut (or should it be cut at all?), and so on. There are also a host of different jobs in a production: acting, lighting, costumes, and front-of-house.

You could also try shorter versions of the play (or of parts of it). A useful approach is to put on a version of the play that lasts a very short time, perhaps twenty minutes. This could be done with a combination of mime, narration and dialogue from the play, and music and dance. You would need to develop a script first, and then work in groups on the different scenes. The final production could be to younger children, perhaps in their schools.

An even shorter version could be created by selecting some of the key speeches/lines/images in the play, and performing them as a group. You could combine choral (group) reading, different parts being read by different people, and music. This would give an aural version of the play, though it could be combined with mime and/or tableaux (or still photographs). Perhaps the shortest version of all would be tableaux of the four to six key moments in the play (as you see them). This is something you could easily do in the classroom.

As some of the activities suggest, with a comedy, it's often not what you do, but the way that you do it which is important. Experiments with different ways of acting out any part of the play, or trying out various interpretations of a character are valuable ways of exploring the play. Your group can pick its own section of the play (or a character) and experiment with how the humour can be brought out.

'The minute you say "fairy" to people, they think they know exactly what it is – and they're outraged if they don't get it.'

(About Titania and Oberon) 'It's power games, and sex is the first weapon they use against each other.' Siobhan Redmond

Some people have very clear ideas about the fairies on stage. Deciding how to present the fairies is vital to how you present the play. Pick a scene from the play and produce it in a number of different ways, with different kinds of fairies. This will bring out different ways of looking at the fairies and the fairy world, and different ways of looking at the play itself.

'The more serious the Mechanicals are about their play, the more intent and earnest, the funnier the result is. It's easy to get a bit self-indulgent when performing their play. But to them it is the most serious and terrifying thing, they're going to the palace to perform.' Karl James (Snug in the Renaissance Theatre Company production)

'I've played so many people like that who are bigheaded or obsessive. I always try and see their problems and their point of view. Bottom's just a little fish in a little pond who puffs himself up – which is what comedy is all about.' Richard Briers (Bottom in the same production)

One of the best sections of the play to explore is the Mechanicals' play in Act 5. There are a host of possibilities here, so don't be limited by these suggestions. The whole play can be produced as it stands. Or it can be changed in a variety of ways – modern comments on the production from another audience, miming only, re-written in the language of some sub-culture (the greasers' play, the American version, and so on), or even just limited to the Mechanicals' play, or part of the play. Perhaps the experimental approaches could come first: miming, then some degree of cutting/re-writing, and then a 'full' production. But even when you are tackling a 'full' production, keep experimenting. Try different versions (grimly determined to do their best, frightened by the whole experience of acting in front of the Court, or totally over-the-top). It would be useful to compare how *your* play develops with the way the Mechanicals' play develops in rehearsal.

Visually, the play is one of the most interesting of all Shakespeare's plays, and this could lead to a variety of activities. Drawing (and creating) a set and scenery, costume design, and posters for the play is an excellent way of developing your ideas, either as a group or on your own. Still photographs (or other visual presentations) of moments in a production offer another valuable means of engaging with the visual side of the play. Another good technique is the use of video, which offers a permanent record of improvisation and performance that can be discussed (and edited). Although video takes much more time than performing to an audience, it is worthwhile exploring the play in this way.

Going to see a production (or even seeing a film or television version of the play) is essential. The main thing is to watch and enjoy the play, but there are related activities you might consider. Perhaps you might study one key character, and then follow that character through the performance. Or you might develop your idea of the fairies and sets, and then compare them with those used in the production. You might even read and discuss reviews before you go, and then comment on their accuracy after you've seen the play.

After a drawing illustrating the play. Compare this with page 74.

Young lovers and courtship

The importance of courtship and marriage in the play led many people to think *A Midsummer Night's Dream* was written as an entertainment for an aristocratic wedding, but this is almost certainly not true. But it is about love and relationships. Compare the attitude to love and relationships in the play with the attitude among your friends, your parents, and different groups in society today. Start by comparing the young lovers in the play with any you may know.

One of the ideas in the play is that there is a difference between 'doting' and 'love', something like the distinction between fancying someone (being physically attracted to them) and loving them. But the play also presents 'love' as a kind of madness, a way of looking at someone that is like magic (or, at least, irrational). These days love is often presented as an extremely good thing, but in the play 'reason and love keep little company together'. Considering lots of different examples, look at what love means today and what it seems to mean in the play. You could then make a display – perhaps using photographs and illustrations – to show the differences (and similarities). What is your own view of love?

But of course the play revolves around the conflicts in relationships as well as love. For each relationship, identify the causes of the conflicts (even think about Pyramus and Thisbe, although the Mechanicals' play unintentionally mocks their situation, just as Shakespeare seems to be mocking the lovers in his play). Explain your view of how these conflicts are resolved, and whether the characters have changed by the end of the play.

Another way of looking at this is to consider how different the relationships appear at different points in the play. For each relationship pick a moment in the wood to act out, and then a moment from Act 4 or 5. Then describe the feelings that seem to be dominant in the wood, and compare them to the feelings dominant in Act 4 or 5. Some people think the wood was a place where the lovers could really display their emotions (both love *and* hate), away from the restrictions of law, society and their parents. How does this view compare with what you have found?

Patterns or structures

There are many patterns in the play. Find as many as you can. For example, there are the different relationships between the lovers (who loves who at different points – refer to the activities). There are also patterns in the play as a whole to do with places, time of day (or night), characters (and the stereotypes associated with different classes), and other things, including even the division of the play into five acts. For each of the patterns you discover, write down as many features associated with the pattern as you can find.

Of course just finding a pattern isn't enough. Take the pattern of the play in terms of place (palace—wood—palace). Your list of features of this pattern could make you think the palace was associated with reason and the wood with emotion. But there is a lot of emotion in the scenes in the palace. The palace is the mortal world, and the wood the fairy world – but the fairies do appear in the palace at the end of the play. Use your list of features associated with each pattern to interpret the pattern, but don't feel there has to be just one 'right' answer.

There are other kinds of pattern you could look for:

- patterns of power (men and women, mortals and fairies, and so on),
- patterns of images (day and night, Bottom and asses, and so on), and even
- patterns of experiences (the experience of the lovers and Bottom in the wood creates a sense of growing unreality for them and the audience, for example)
- patterns of appearance versus reality.

After finding as many patterns as you can and trying to interpret them, see if the patterns themselves fit together somehow. You could make charts or diagrams to show your ideas. Don't worry if you don't come to any final conclusions – perhaps there aren't any. It's exploring how the whole play is structured that matters.

Shakespeare's language

Make displays that will put across what you feel are some of the most important features of Shakespeare's language. Look at the 'Watch your language' activities on pages 30 and 56 for ideas, but include other things, such as:

- famous/favourite lines from the play
- photographs of acting activities next to the lines from the script
- your own attempts at writing like Shakespeare
- drawings of Shakespeare's verbal 'pictures' opposite his verse
- examples of different kinds of word-play and humour.

Different fonts (if you're using a computer to print) can help make your displays interesting.

Match the forms of the writing with the characters (lyrics for the fairies, prose for the Mechanicals, and so on), explaining what you think the connection is between the characters and the form. Experiment with the forms Shakespeare uses, writing your own blank verse, couplets, lyrics and prose. Link the kind of language to the characters and forms (the Mechanicals use working people's language in prose, the Court use middle-class language and blank verse, and so on). Write your own prose and verse this way, where the kind of language fits the character and form. Finally, the Mechanicals' play is a parody of bad plays in Shakespeare's day: write your own parody of part of *A Midsummer Night's Dream*.

Writing is, in part, creating images with words. Acting creates images too (but on stage). Make a display of what you feel are the key images in the play, using photographs and drawings for the acting images, and including the key images in words.

The play is full of references to gods, mythical characters (such as Titania, Puck, Theseus and others), and stories from other literature (such as Pyramus and Thisbe, or a man being transformed into an ass). Does that mean the play is just a myth or dream made up from other myths and dreams? Some people think the more real literature is on the surface, the better it is. Others think the use of myths and stories in this play helps establish the importance of imagination in our lives. Compare this play with other literature you know, especially its language.

Ideas in – and out of – the play

Like exploring patterns in *A Midsummer Night's Dream* you can explore ideas related to it. In the play, 'imagination' is the mind's ability to create or change what it perceives (especially when the person is in love). Imagination is also what creates the audience's vision – and even the author's.

There are other interesting ideas about the play. One is based on the many festivals in which lovers and others were allowed to do things normally forbidden (like being alone in the woods all night). Festivals (like holidays today) were a kind of release from the pressures of normal life, after which normal life seemed better, both for the society and the individual – or so the theory suggested. Another idea suggests that the fairies represent natural forces (both in the world and in the minds of the characters), as opposed to laws and reason. Using your work on patterns, invent your own theories or ideas.

The trouble with most theories is they seem to answer some of the questions, but not all of them. For example, imagination is criticised in Theseus' speech in 5.1.2–22, and mocked in the lovers' changes of partners, but the Mechanicals' lack of imagination is also mocked. Or Puck thinks 'what fools these Mortals be', but Oberon and Titania (and Puck himself) hardly behave in a sensible way all the time. In thinking about the play, it is possible to 'de-construct it' – to pull it apart looking for ideas and beliefs – but none of these ideas is necessarily valid, because they only come from characters who are 'visions', 'shadows', the product of Shakespeare's and our own imagination. But thinking about these ideas – and the problems with such ideas and theories – can help you look at the play in new ways.

It isn't the ideas that matter most, however, it's the play itself, the performances you are in and see. It's the experience of being involved as part of an audience or part of the play. And it's the direct contact with Shakespeare himself, hearing his words and seeing his play despite the 400 years that have passed:

So, good night unto you all.
Give me your hands, if we be friends,
And Robin shall restore amends.

William Shakespeare 1564–1616

1564 Born Stratford-upon-Avon, eldest son of John and Mary Shakespeare.
1582 Married to Anne Hathaway of Shottery, near Stratford.
1583 Daughter, Susanna, born.
1585 Twins, son and daughter, Hamnet and Judith, born.
1592 First mention of Shakespeare in London. Robert Greene, another playwright, described Shakespeare as 'an upstart crow beautified with our feathers . . .'. Greene seems to have been jealous of Shakespeare. He mocked Shakespeare's name, calling him 'the only Shake-scene in a country' (presumably because Shakespeare was writing successful plays).
1595 A shareholder in 'The Lord Chamberlain's Men', an acting company that became extremely popular.
1596 Son Hamnet died, aged eleven.
Father, John, granted arms (acknowledged as a gentleman).
1597 Bought New Place, the grandest house in Stratford.
1598 Acted in Ben Jonson's *Every Man in His Humour*.
1599 Globe Theatre opens on Bankside. Performances in the open air.
1601 Father, John, dies.
1603 James I granted Shakespeare's company a royal patent: 'The Lord Chamberlain's Men' became 'The King's Men' and played about twelve performances each year at court.
1607 Daughter, Susanna, marries Dr John Hall.
1608 Mother, Mary, dies.
1609 'The King's Men' begin performing indoors at Blackfriars Theatre.
1610 Probably returned from London to live in Stratford.
1616 Daughter, Judith, marries Thomas Quiney.
Died. Buried in Holy Trinity Church, Stratford-upon-Avon.

The plays and poems
(no one knows exactly when he wrote each play)

1589–1595 *The Two Gentlemen of Verona, The Taming of the Shrew, First, Second and Third Parts of King Henry VI, Titus Andronicus, King Richard III, The Comedy of Errors, Love's Labour's Lost, A Midsummer Night's Dream, Romeo and Juliet, King Richard II* (and the long poems *Venus and Adonis* and *The Rape of Lucrece*).

1596–1599 *King John, The Merchant of Venice, First and Second Parts of King Henry IV, The Merry Wives of Windsor, Much Ado About Nothing, King Henry V, Julius Caesar* (and probably the *Sonnets*).

1600–1605 *As You Like It, Hamlet, Twelfth Night, Troilus and Cressida, Measure for Measure, Othello, All's Well That Ends Well, Timon of Athens, King Lear.*

1606–1611 *Macbeth, Antony and Cleopatra, Pericles, Coriolanus, The Winter's Tale, Cymbeline, The Tempest.*

1613 *King Henry VIII, The Two Noble Kinsmen* (both probably with John Fletcher)

1623 Shakespeare's plays published as a collection (now called the First Folio).